Praise for Wild Dancing

"Janice Edwards knows the touch of the Holy deep in the core of her being, and from this core of authentic experience she speaks of the sacred dynamic underpinning all that is. She knows at first hand how life can break open all our defenses, leaving us trembling in the hands of God, where at last we discover who we truly are. Her experience of the mystical is of a powerful active presence drawing her ever more deeply into the wild dancing that is unafraid to weave into itself the darkest recesses of human experience: whether critical illness, depression, sexual abuse, the trauma of terrorist attack, or the systemic evil of violent oppression, rape, and murder. In the worst that we can experience or imagine, 'love brings goodness out of evil's madness,' and in the power of this mystery, everything is being drawn into the heart of resurrection. This is a book to bring genuine hope into a world overshadowed by despair."

—MARGARET SILF
Writer and Retreat-Giver

"I was immediately drawn to Sister Janice Edwards's book. What shall we call an experience of near-life healing whereby everything is as we remember it, but our relationship to the world is utterly changed? I think Janice Edwards's book belongs to a genre we have yet to name adequately. It is the testimony of someone who understands that the Ill and the Well do not inhabit separate worlds, but the same world. Though perhaps it is only those who have passed through illness—including the illness of giving birth—who are awakened to the mystery of communion that Sister Janice describes."

—RICHARD RODRIGUEZ
Author of *Brown: The Last Discovery of America*

"This is a rare and original book, full of wisdom about the spiritual life, human suffering, prayer, dark contemplation as well as light, and experiences of uni
and with God. As a first-perso
transparent, yet other-centered,
of the most complex of human
and all that God's love holds in b

author's experience together with the spiritual experience of others, both historical and contemporary. Universal markers are delicately, almost imperceptibly, drawn from spiritual theologies and even science. Deeply serious, it remains down to earth with intermittent and surprising sparkles of humor. Beautifully written, it is above all a story, and an interpretation of a story, that rings true."

—MARGARET FARLEY, RSM
Gilbert L. Stark Professor Emerita of Christian Ethics,
Yale University Divinity School

"As I read Sr. Janice Edwards's new book, I began to wonder if Pierre Teilhard de Chardin himself had commissioned her to write it. Teilhard wrote extensively of a mystical love suffusing the universe, but over the years some scholars have criticized his vision as being too optimistic, as being unable to deal effectively with the harsh realities of pain and evil. Enter Janice Edwards and her wonderful Wild Dancing. Her vision of love is just as cosmic as Teilhard's, but it is also a love that is clearly stronger than debilitating disease, than rape, than injustice, than the most intense physical suffering, all of which she has known personally. With her celebration of her discovery of a nondual spirituality, Sr. Janice Edwards invites us to join the central action of the universe, that sometimes terrifying but ultimately magnificent journey into becoming Love Itself."

—BRIAN THOMAS SWIMME, PhD
Professor of Cosmology, California Institute of Integral Studies, San Francisco

"As a seasoned spiritual director, Janice Edwards, RSM, seamlessly weaves her spiritual journey, those of her directees, and a contemporary vision of the contemplative life. She invites us through her own spiritual awakening and healing into the power to contemplate both the light and shadowy aspects of Reality, to be transformed into Love and the Dance of Life. This is a book of hope and vision and most profoundly experience. She decontaminates old god imagery and heals us as we read. A must for anyone seriously on the spiritual journey!"

—DON BISSON, FMS, D.Min.
Formator of Spiritual Directors

Wild Dancing

Wild Dancing

EMBRACED BY UNTAMED LOVE

JANICE EDWARDS, RSM

Dear Anne

I have appreciated you & your great journey & your great Love of Mercy for quite a while.

May the God who dances across this cover draw you

BROOKVILLE BOOKS

& all of us into her wildly free Dance of the universe

Love – Janice

Published by Brookville Books
PO Box 96
Sea Cliff, NY 11579

ISBN 13: 978-0-87957-022-4
ISBN 10: 0-87957-022-9
Printed in the United States of America
Signature Book Printing, www.sbpbooks.com

10 9 8 7 6 5 4 3 2 1

I dedicate this book to my parents, Marie Schairer Edwards and George W. Edwards. Without your Love, faith, creativity, and integrity, there would be no book and, more importantly, no joy in my heart.

I also dedicate it to all sisters, associates, companions, and co-workers in Mercy around the world. Being one with you in Catherine McAuley's Dance animates each day of my life.

Contents

Foreword

Wild Dancing is appearing at exactly the time it is most needed in our Western contemplative tradition. It is a daring book because its author courageously offers to her reading public a very personal journey of mystical discovery and intimate spiritual, physical, and emotional experience. Writing in a deeply personal and accessible style, Janice Edwards, a very experienced spiritual director, describes her deepest experience with God/Jesus whom she names "Wild Dancing" or more simply "Love." She traces this lifelong movement in Love within her until it becomes inseparable from herself in deeply unitive and transforming contemplative experience. Drawing on important themes in spirituality, theology, and cosmology in the last fifty years, she shows how they supported her experience and opened her understanding to what she was experiencing. These sources are used sparingly but may serve as mentors for those who read her narrative of spiritual transformation and who seek more guidance for their own journeys from writers like Thomas Berry, Brian Swimme, Teilhard de Chardin, Thomas Merton, William Connolly, Constance FitzGerald, and classical medieval Christian mystics like Julian of Norwich and John Ruusbroec.

Janice begins her riveting, first-person narrative with life-threatening and saving brain surgery, and the extreme physical incapacitation that immediately followed this surgery. Then she writes about how she awakened from the anesthesia into the total embrace of an untamed Love that she recognized as God. The damage to one hemisphere of her brain from her nonmalignant tumor and the subsequent surgery became the initiating event through which she experienced Love in its most intimate and all-embracing form, and she responded to it with all of her self. She takes us on her journey through the physical and emotional healing that follows, but this breakthrough into God as nothing but all-embracing Love dancing within and about her becomes the touchstone for the rest of the narrative. Unlike many first-person accounts of deeply significant experiences, Janice makes the connection between her own experience of Love and the ways she met this same Love moving in and through the lives of many of her directees. She connects her personal story with those of others for the purpose of inviting all of her readers into their unique experience of God's revelation to her. When we, as readers, glimpse Love's way with her directees and the public narratives of several other men and women, we recognize she is telling a story that is both universal and deeply personal, and that we, too, can participate in Love's Dancing.

This is no journey for the faint-hearted. Janice's personal journey includes not only her life-changing experience of brain surgery and its aftermath, but also a unique insight into the journey of Roman Catholic Sisters of Mercy from Vatican II to the present from the perspective of both membership and leadership. And she recounts her healing journey from childhood sexual abuse. She connects the suffering she experienced with the suffering of others, such as the family members of those killed in the Twin Towers on September 11 and the tortured and abused religious women killed by graduates of the School of the Americas. Love's Wild Dancing is present even here in the midst of great suffering and unspeakable evil just as poignantly as Love dances through the grand beauty of her particular sacred landscape, Monhegan Island in Maine. In these lyrical pages where Janice describes her experience of Love in moments of quiet contemplation, kayaking gently offshore, or observing the mysterious intricacy of nature through the lens of her camera, we glimpse the oneness of Love with all of creation and the environment of communion with Love and one another to which we are all called and for which we long consciously or unconsciously. Rarely does a writer on contemplative experience connect both the beauty and the pain of existence in this God-soaked world so poignantly and with the hope to which Julian of Norwich's teaching points, "All shall be well." In this narrative, these words resonate as utterly true precisely because she holds both unspeakably intimate Love together with equally unutterable human evil and the suffering it creates.

This book is also timely. In my own practice of spiritual direction, and in several other sources, there is a new convergence arising, particularly although not exclusively in the experience of contemplative women, that God is Love, and that Love's ways with us are deeply intimate, unique, yet are not impeded by the specific suffering we undergo, the evil we confront, or the challenges we face. Even more that that, Love is inviting, enticing, desirous of reciprocity and response in this communion of being that we are and that is our deepest fulfillment. This is occurring precisely at a time when there is an upsurgence of a harsh and divisive fundamentalism among many religious traditions that claims to speak for and propagates a judgmental, punishing, alienating god who is nothing more than the projection of our own fears and desire to punish. Julian of Norwich discovered God is wholly Love in fourteenth-century Norwich; Brother Emmanuel of Taize recently writes of this Love in *Love, Imperfectly Known*; and Janice Edwards gives us this exquisite narrative of Love's ways, which simply invites us into deep communion with Love and everything else that is in her powerful and evocative narrative. Although she clearly states that this book is not a book about how to pray, anyone who does pray and who has any intimation of the reality that opens to those who pray with heart and mind open will also experience much encouragement for their own forays into Love's intimate communion and Wild Dancing.

Janet K. Ruffing, RSM, PhD

Professor of the Practice of Spirituality and Ministerial Leadership, Yale Divinity School, and author of *To Tell the Sacred Tale: Spiritual Direction and Narrative* (Paulist, 2011).

Acknowledgments

While I was writing this book, many people supported my contemplation of Love's Dance, and I am profoundly grateful to all of them.

My parents, Marie and George, are now in their early nineties. My experience of God's all-embracing Love originates in their loving fidelity to each other, my brothers, and me.

My brothers, Jeff and Scott, have encouraged me throughout. I am blessed to have these very good men in my life. Cindy, my sister–in-law, and my nieces, Rachel, Sarah, and Wren, have often expressed interest in my work. Cindy and Wren also edited my manuscript, and I benefited greatly from their literary creativity.

While I was working on this project, Sharon Donohue, Mariann Mahon, Christine McCann, Diane Szubrowski, and Patricia Vetrano were congregational leaders for the Sisters of Mercy. They always trusted that I was following God's inspiration and timeline to the best of my ability. Theresina Flannery, Elizabeth O'Hara, Mildred Rossiter, and Mary Ruane were members of the Sisters of Mercy leadership team with me from from 1986 to 1990. Their understanding and compassion toward me as I journeyed through the hell described in Chapters 10 and 11 made that suffering much easier to bear.

Clifford Browder, an author and editor, generously guided my writing throughout. I learned a great deal about creating and publishing a book from his steady and competent advice. His editing, encouragement, and friendship made the sometimes tedious process of finishing this project possible.

Barry and Louise Young's ongoing conviction that I could create a book about God's incredible Love fostered my ability to do so. Louise's refined listening, exceptional creativity, and patient editing empowered my writing. Barry's staunch commitment to this project provided the financial resources needed for it. Their steadfast friendship astounds and humbles me.

I also thank Kari Keyock. Louise Young and her daughter,

Kari, took one of my photographs of Monhegan Island and created the beautiful and meaningful cover of this book.

Toward the end of this process William Barry, SJ, gave my manuscript a thorough editing. This creation is more reader-friendly because of his careful deletions, wise comments, and generous spirit. Vinita Wright, an editor at Loyola Press, also offered invaluable insights in this last phase.

Elizabeth Daniels Anton, George and Janet Bickford, Malcolm and Rebecca Briggs, Valerie and Robert Downing, Marilyn McDonald, Mary McLear, John Walker, and Catherine Warshaw-Garguilo generously contributed the finances needed for my writing. Because of them, my contemplation of Monhegan Island highlights God's earthy Dance there and throughout our universe. Monsignor Casimir Ladzinski and the Church of the Sacred Heart in Bayhead, N.J., donated funds to the Sisters of Mercy for the first publication of this book. No words sufficiently express my gratitude for the largesse of these donors.

Many Sisters of Mercy have encouraged me while writing. Mary Bilderback, Mary Paula Cancieene, Moira Kenny, Patricia Kenny, Maria Cordis Richey, Carol Rittner, Janet Ruffing, Kathleen Sonnie, and Margaret Taylor offered advice on a chapter or two, and Sheila Carney, Lisa Gambacorto, and Kathleen Smith gave input on numerous chapters. Sisters' kind words regarding this book often boosted my morale. In some ways the last few years of this adventure were the most difficult, so I am especially grateful to the sisters with whom I have lived during that time: Rosemary Hudak, Mary Mason, and Vida O'Leary.

Three Sisters of Mercy from Portland, Maine, and three from Worcester, Massachusetts, provided hospitality and so much more as I traveled from New Jersey to Monhegan Island, Maine, each year. Sisters Mary Matthew Blanchard, Margaret Ann Brown, Rita Mary Hamel, Jacqueline Moreau, Patricia Pora, and Kathleen Smith generously shared hospitality and friendship during these trips. In addition, the Religious of the Assumption, also in Worcester, have offered me generous hospitality on these trips.

I am thankful to Ted Dunn and Beth Lipsmeyer for their

insightful editing during the early stages of my writing. Because of their careful advice, I changed some important aspects of my writing.

Monhegan's islanders and visitors have welcomed me to this rustic but magnificent piece of earth. Barbara Hitchcock provided a home, friendship, and much more. Sylvia Alberts, Harry T. Bone, Tom and Josephine Martin, Helen Prince, Ray Steiniford, Beth Van Houten, and many others offered artistic encouragement and great conversation while I resided on Monhegan. After reading my manuscript, Helen Prince gave an especially caring and careful response to it.

My early writing of this book coincided with the horrendous September 11th attack on the World Trade Center. As I contemplated that horror, I was drawn to write about Welles Crowther, a twenty-four-year-old volunteer firefighter, who worked full time at Sandler O'Neill & Partners on the 104th floor of the World Trade Center. This young man escaped from the South Tower, returned to rescue at least a dozen people, and finally died when the South Tower collapsed. Quite sadly, during my final editing, I had to let go of my writing about him, because it no longer fit within the entire manuscript. But I am still moved by his astonishing Love that day, so I honor Welles by mentioning him here. I also thank his mother, Alison Crowther, for generously introducing me to her son and Ling Young and Judy Wein for telling me about their rescue by Welles, who, on that dreadful day, was also known as the "man in the red bandana." I continue to contemplate the lives, deaths, and self-sacrifice of so many people during that time. I pray to those who died and for the families who lost so much.

I valued the dedicated support, competence, creativity, and friendliness of Charles and Dan Roth, my publishers, and Teresa Jesionowski, my editor, as we prepared my manuscript for publication. I am most grateful to Karen Doyle, SSJ, for introducing me to Charles Roth. Without her caring introduction, I might have never connected with these fine people.

Because of their insight into the spirit of my writing, I am deeply heartened by the foreword written by Janet Ruffing, RSM and the endorsement of Margaret Farley, RSM. Likewise, the appraisals of Donald Bisson, Richard Rodriguez, Margaret Silf, and Brian Swimme lifted my spirit.

I am grateful for the support I have received in many peer-supervision groups. Nancy Brubaker, Barbara Martel, Marcus Pomeroy, Ellie Stratton, Elizabeth Sweeney, and Barry Young were committed members of one such group, and their deep love of the field of spiritual direction moves me still.

At varied times, William Barry, Madeline Birmingham, James Borbely, William Connolly, Katherine Fitzgerald, Anne Harvey, Margaret Luby, Kathleen McAlpin, and my classmates at the former Center for Religious Development in Cambridge, Massachusetts, have offered me either spiritual direction or supervision. I have been given the finest guides for contemplating Love, the grandest adventure that I know.

Wild Dancing

Introduction

At the age of forty-three I experienced brain surgery to remove a benign but very destructive brain tumor. When the doctors woke me after three days of anesthesia, a friend came to visit. I could have talked about an utterly bedridden body and much impairment, but instead I spoke about Love and its communion. My body was disabled, yet my spirit soared. Your spirit can also soar.

Love

The incredible Love that I met when I woke from anesthesia is the heart of this book. I no longer see Love as one human emotion among others, nor solely as the possession of human beings. I have learned that Love is the sole invincible and all-embracing force of the universe. The God that dances through this book is a person and a cosmic energy that livens and leavens everything and everyone. By always capitalizing the noun Love, I remind myself and you that God is Love and Love is God. I am most comfortable using the words "Love," "God," and "Dance" to represent the sacred dimension of the universe. As you read this book, I hope you enrich my descriptions by substituting your own terms for this mystery that envelops us all.

Our frequent use of the word *Love* can weaken it, so I use the words *wild* and *untamed* to accentuate the extraordinary nature of its Dance. The Love that I met when I awakened from anesthesia and meet when I offer spiritual direction to others is anything but conventional, predictable, and controllable. A sacred presence moves through the universe; this untamed presence explodes conceptual categories, fulfills passionate desires, and surpasses our wildest dreams. Since my awakening, I feel compelled to share this force that I sense pulsing through the universe and stake everything on the Dance I experience.

Contemplation

Wild Dancing revolves around Love, our capacity to contemplate it, and its ability to change us. Contemplation is an extremely important, innately human, and often underrated capability, and I let our experience of it describe its meaning. Have you ever experienced overwhelming joy while walking through a forest or while feeling your newborn child grip your finger? If so, you have experienced contemplation and the incredible Love it exposes. Observing a sunset or a smile can turn into a long look, tender embrace, or deep awareness, and this type of meditation is always an encounter with Love. These loving connections can be slow and calm or swift and wild.

This book revolves around experiences like these. It is not a "how to" book about contemplation; others have written fine books with procedures that help us pray.[1] Because contemplation is more like an experience than a concept, a happening than a plan, and a gift than a feat, some of us find fostering experiences of God more helpful than talking about them. I hope that telling stories and conveying experiences will arouse your awareness of Love's presence within and around you. Because I focus on encounters with rather than explanations of God, you may find perusing any chapter more fulfilling than reading the book from start to finish.

Encountering Love also changes us, and, over time, immersion in Love transforms us in radical ways. As the chapters progress we see how contemplating God reveals communion, intensifies Love, focuses desire, refines vulnerability, transfigures suffering, stirs protest, and gradually exposes the union of heaven and earth. All the while, God is convincing us of God's words to Julian of Norwich, "All shall be well." The life-changing narratives of lovers of Monhegan Island, churchwomen in El Salvador, victims of September 11th, and my own recovery stories make of this book an ode to contemplative transformation.

As prayer becomes a lifetime practice, Love uses it to make us more like itself. Sometimes contemplation is a look, and always it is an encounter and an embrace. Prayer can include conversion, consolation, pain, protest, or all of these experienced as one. This gazing is always an intimacy that stirs our depth and reveals our connection with everything. The tension created as God's unlimited Love rubs against our limited Love gradually transforms us. Sooner or later, dwelling on another becomes a Dance where two become one, and we no longer know who is contemplating whom. Untamed Love pulls us into its wildly free Dance of the universe. Then, our Love becomes a little more like God's, and all that we see is grand diversity held as one.

Love's Stories

At first my new awareness of Love's communion overwhelmed me, but its development had been years in the making. In 1965 I had joined the Sisters of Mercy, a Roman Catholic community of women religious. Developing a personal and communal spirituality is a central focus in the lives of women and men religious, so some years later I began studying and teaching spirituality in universities and spirituality centers, and soon this field of study became my life. Nearly forty years of offering spiritual direction to others influences every story I tell in this book.

Chapters 1 through 3 reveal how Love used brain surgery to show me that it holds everything in an all-inclusive communion. Chapters 4 through 6 show how contemplating God intensifies our Love and deepens our relationships. Narratives about a father and son at the beach, a young priest named Mike, and a nature lover named Tom reveal that we are all siblings in Love's untamed Dance.

Chapter 7 uses a directee's and my own search for fulfillment and the cosmologist Brian Swimme's experience of gravity to highlight how God attracts everything and everyone and uses our desires to help us pray. In Chapters 8 and 9 we watch prayer refine vulnerability. As Marian Fontana wrestled with the profound grief of losing her firefighter husband on September 11th, and as I recovered from the vulnerability of severe brain surgery, we contemplate God using limitation to strengthen our

Love and humility.

Sometimes prayer is extremely difficult. Chapters 10 through 13 introduce dark contemplation. Though the words *dark contemplation* refer to varied prayer experiences in the Christian spiritual tradition, I use them to signify recovery from evil's horrid destruction. I share stories about my adult recovery from childhood sexual abuse and about the rape and murder of four American churchwomen by the Salvadoran military in 1980. Therein we contemplate Love as it uses contemporary protests against violence to resurrect the ongoing power of these churchwomen. I also describe how God used their rape in 1980 to heal me of my own decades later. During dark contemplation we experience the radical nature of untamed Love.

In the conclusion we witness contemplation's power to revive us. This chapter's ode to awesome wonder emphasizes that "All manner of thing shall be well."[2]

Earth and Heaven Dancing

Before my surgery I saw and taught spirituality mostly as a human phenomenon. Then came brain surgery and its radical transformation. After that I saw spirituality, or the Love within us, as a far grander venture, a human, earth, and cosmic experience. Deep within creation, I perceived Love dancing everything and everyone freely and wildly; never again could I speak or write solely about human spirituality.

Monhegan Island, a small island off mid-coast Maine, grounds my experience of earth spirituality and plays a prominent role in this book. This rustic and magnificent piece of earth attracts people from around the world. Late in 1991 a friend and I traveled to this small island. During that two-day visit, Monhegan embraced me far more powerfully than I understood. Since my first visit to this amazing place, I have learned with Thomas Merton that "it is essential to experience all the times and moods of one good place."[3] Monhegan has taught me much about earth spirituality. There, Love moves amid earth and soil, rock and surf, summer people and islanders.

***

I have found only two ladyslippers on Monhegan. Contemplating this lovely, elusive flower would cultivate spirituality in the most hardened skeptic. I found these flowers after seven years of searching, and wrote a few words in their honor. Will you join me in their Dance?

> With tripod and lens, I prostrate before you.
> My lens magnifies your beauty.
> Words fail, my most sensitive lens falters.
> Contemplation.
> Experience communes.
> My response, a deeply humble bow.
> Communion.
> Earth and heaven are one.
> Gotta Dance!

Notes

1 I value *God and You, Prayer as a Personal Relationship* by William Barry, SJ, *Experiencing God's Tremendous Love* by Maureen Conroy, RSM, *Close to the Heart* and *At Sea with God* by Margaret Silf as practical guides for prayer.

2 Julian of Norwich, *The Showings of Julian of Norwich*, trans. Denise N. Baker (New York: W. W. Norton, 2005), 44.

3 Thomas Merton, *Conjectures of a Guilty Bystander* (New York: Doubleday, 1966), 179.

1

Brain Surgery

Dealing with the reality of brain surgery could have been a nightmare, but life's Dance gave it an unpredictable twist. God's great-hearted Love sustained me through the ups and downs of preparing for major surgery. Contemplating Love made all the difference.

Bad News

I was excited as I moved to Philadelphia in September of 1990 to begin a new ministry. Chestnut Hill College in Philadelphia had just established two master's degree programs in holistic spirituality and spiritual direction. I had been hired to teach spirituality courses and create a spiritual direction practicum.

But I began to experience a ringing in my ear and an intermittent dizziness in my brain. Within two weeks of my initial consultation with Dr. Max Ronis, I had completed the battery of tests he ordered and was again sitting in his office waiting for the results. Because I was a healthy forty-two-year-old who had never experienced anything life threatening, I relaxed while I waited. I assumed this was a minor ailment that could be reversed with medication. While waiting, I read a pamphlet about maladies that affected hearing and balance. It contained brief descriptions of minor and major ailments. Tinnitus was less serious; Ménière's disease and acoustic neuromas were more serious. Ménière's disease sounded terrible to me, with its chronic bouts of spinning, accompanied by nausea, vomiting, or sweating. I noted briefly that acoustic neuromas necessitated life-threatening brain surgery.

I read this booklet merely to pass the time. After all, how serious could ringing in the ear be? And the dizzy sensation was not continuous. When Dr. Ronis arrived in the examination room, he was as friendly as he had been during the previous visit. After some engaging conversation, he came to the point, "Sister, I'm very sorry to say that you have an acoustic neuroma." I vaguely recalled reading that brain surgery was required to remove these tumors, but Ménière's disease still sounded worse. I said in response, "Well, at least I don't have Ménière's disease." He became quite serious then. "Sister, I don't think you understand what I've said. I wish you had Ménière's disease."

He explained that acoustic neuromas are benign brain tumors that grow slowly but must be completely removed because they gradually destroy vital functions. They grow on the eighth cranial nerve, which enables hearing and balance on the right side of the brain. That explained my difficulties with ringing and balance. Now doctors can use less invasive surgery to remove these tumors, but in 1990 this operation was still quite destructive. But this tumor's symptoms were revealing themselves early, so it was smaller than some acoustic neuromas. He added that the surgeon might be able to operate without seriously damaging the nearby nerves.

At the end of our visit, he took me by the hand, and led me to the receptionist and asked her to make an appointment for me with Dr. William Bucheit, a neurosurgeon. As he held my hand throughout the walk, I said to myself, "This must be serious." I was emotionally numb at first. I had never experienced surgery of any kind; now I needed serious brain surgery. The surgery was especially sensitive, because it would occur close to the brain stem, the hub of the central nervous system. In order to remove the tumor, the surgeon's implements would move amid the cranial nerves, a cluster of juxtaposed, indispensable nerves on each side of the brain.

Because acoustic neuromas grow slowly, the timing of the surgery was elective. Since I was teaching at the time, I decided to have the surgery in mid-December, after the semester ended. During the next few weeks, as I talked with family and friends, visited the neurosurgeon, and read more about acoustic neuromas, the reality began to affect me. I had nearly three months to prepare for the surgery. During those months I experienced the ups and downs that accompany the expectation of formidable surgery. Paying attention to God's presence in these ups and downs was sometimes easy and sometimes quite difficult.

Destructive Surgery

During the early weeks after the diagnosis, doctors helped me understand the surgery for which I was preparing. A booklet I was given was straightforward without being dramatic. Essentially it said that in order to save my life, I would have to undergo fairly destructive surgery. It delineated the temporary and permanent effects this operation might have on my body. These facts forced me to internalize its harsh reality.

The booklet said there was a very low chance of paralysis or death, and the doctors assured me I had little to worry about in this area because of my youth and good health. Through reading and conversations I gradually determined which outcomes might affect me. Since the tumor was small, the doctors said they would try to remove it without destroying the hearing and balance functions on the right side of my brain. They were pretty sure they could salvage the seventh cranial nerve, which was extremely close to the eighth. This nerve controls some facial muscles and the varied functions of the eyelids on the right side. The doctors stressed that I would not be able to do any work for at least four months after the surgery. Bed rest would foster needed healing, and besides I would be very tired. So I planned to stay at the health-care facility of the Sisters of Mercy for those months.

Emotions Intensify

I have forgotten most of the events that provoked anxiety and fear prior to the surgery, but a few have stayed with me. In the early 1990s computers were becoming a part of everyday life. Since I had no idea how to use one, I quickly signed up for computer classes at a nearby community college. Ordinarily I enjoy learning new things and, if interested, have good retention skills. But during that first class I could not retain anything, and the simplest tasks became upsetting. I couldn't wait for the end of the class. By the time I reached the car, I was very upset. At first my emotions were jumbled, and then I realized that my distress stemmed from the thought of brain surgery, not participation in a computer class.

As I drove home, my confused emotions became focused fear. The possible outcomes crashed in on me, and everything inside me shook with fear. I had to share my fright with someone, so I called my therapist as soon as I arrived home. I had been seeing Martha, a psychiatrist, for several years, while dealing with some painful events from my childhood, which I write about later in the book. Much of that struggle had diminished. Now I needed her and others to support me with this overwhelming challenge.

Martha helped me gain some perspective. She assured me that most of the listed outcomes would not affect me. The doctors had said they might even be able to save the nerve that controlled my hearing and balance on the right side. As I put the phone down, I noticed God drawing me to herself. I had been utterly focused on my fear, and now, as my emotions quieted, I felt Love attracting me. I had not been able to pay attention to God's allurement while my emotions were so turbulent.

I went to my room, and the gentlest interior pull forced me to sit in my rocker. As I quieted, I sensed Love's presence moving amid any subtle fear that remained. As I paid more attention to this Love and less to my fears, I began to trust it. I vividly remember the emotional shift that occurred between the ride home and my time in the rocker. I moved from being terrified to trusting Love's presence and embrace. Love's gentle movement had quietly and firmly reassured me. Regardless of what happened during and after the surgery, God would be there, holding me tenderly. Nothing mattered half as much as this delicate embrace. This quieting presence also encouraged me to take one day at a time.

Its movement actually held me in the present moment. As I was stilled, I slowly readied myself for bed and quickly fell asleep. When focused on Love, I experienced peace.

Thankfully, ministry distracted me from the difficulty that life had handed me. Nevertheless during the months between my diagnosis and the surgery, I would have more ups and downs. Sometimes my emotions were mild, at other times strong. Sometimes the fear of the unknown seemed overwhelming; at other times the peace that followed it was beyond anything I could have dreamed. The transition between anxious fear and quiet acceptance could be relatively easy or terribly difficult, and I had no way of determining how each struggle would go.

Losing Sight of God

After a few weeks the doctors and I set the surgery for early December of 1990, and I began the required physical preparations. I remember a computerized procedure that mapped my brain. I forget the name of this test but fondly remember the name of the doctor who did the procedure. He introduced himself as Billy Martin, and he explained that this computerized diagram would help the surgeons, nurses, and technicians to be more precise, once their instruments were inside my brain. Precision seemed like a great idea to me! Of all the professionals I met, Billy was the most fun. He integrated wonderful humor with professional competence. Because of him I found great amusement in a serious task.

For this mapping of my brain, I sat in a dark room with electrodes around my head for over an hour. Billy Martin worked with his computers outside the room, and I had to remain still in the darkness. It was morning, and Billy had put me in a great mood, so I was very alert. What were my options for keeping myself still in a pitch-black room for more than an hour? I prayed.

Though I was in that darkness for a long time, little anxiety or fear surfaced. I suppose Billy's upbeat and likable personality helped. Gradually my prayer became very quiet; God and I simply loved each other. Then something occurred that I still recall in detail. There were no images, but I became aware that God and I were within a tunnel that was gradually narrowing. This narrowing was not the least bit frightening. I had a sense that I was dying. God invited me to say good-bye to my family, some friends, and a few community members. Except for saying good-bye to my parents, this letting go was peaceful. While I was focused on Love, most of the good-byes were relatively easy. But saying good-bye to my parents was harder. I was simply not ready to lose them, and in the process of reacting, I lost sight of God.

I fought this good-bye for a bit, but then shared my reactions with Love. Gently and reassuringly, God said, "Look at me. Keep your eyes on me." The sound of his words drew my attention, and I quickly refocused on Love. As I did, I sensed God carrying me again through the last good-bye. As I focused on Love carrying me, I let go and simply trusted him. Then the tunnel fell away, and we were surrounded by deep peace and pervasive light. Once I was in this simple light, I was again connected to my parents. The connection was different than before, but more intimate; I was grateful for this new presence. God and I remained in the simplest peace until the mapping was completed.

Shortly after, I feared that this religious experience might be signaling my coming death from surgery. I often find that I trust God's presence initially, but can sometimes doubt or react negatively to it once I have some distance from the experience. This time the fear was short-lived. The letting go and its results remained with me. God used these ups and downs to deepen my trust.

Fearing Pain and Trusting God

Other instances of trembling before and trusting in Love preceded the surgery. One night in early December I was doing some last-minute shopping for the trip to the hospital and the disability that would follow it. It was an especially dark night. After I accomplished the tasks and began the drive home, I slipped into an inner foreboding, shuddering inside. By this point I was convinced that I would regain my health at some point after the surgery. But the utter lack of control while someone messed with my brain terrified me.

The possibility of physical pain also frightened me. Because I have fibromyalgia, a painful disease that affects many women, I had been dealing with intense pain in various muscles since my late twenties. The thought of surgery adding more pain evoked dread in me. Once I understood the source of this inner darkness, I shared it with Love. During that prayer I remembered how trustworthy God had been throughout my life. I also realized I needed to call the neurosurgeon's office to speak with his nurse. The next day she explained that the surgery would be debilitating, but it would not of itself cause much pain. God's Dance calmed my anxiety.

Delay

All the necessary tests were completed before I arrived at the hospital. I had developed a slight sinus infection the previous day but assumed it would have no effect on the surgery. When I told the surgeon's assistant, everything changed course immediately. This surgery was far too serious; even a slight complication alarmed them enough to postpone the surgery a month. During that month it was my responsibility to get rid of the infection.

Needless to say, I was terribly disappointed. I was ready for that surgery, and God, my family, friends, therapist, and support groups had all enabled this readiness. Now I had a month with one goal: optimum health. Since I was already in the hospital, they did an MRI of my lower back. I often had pain there and wanted to be sure nothing would aggravate long-term bed rest. While lying motionless in the MRI, the Dance revealed the wisdom of the delay. I had been pressuring myself to complete the required medical tests, conclude an academic semester, and prepare for a prolonged stay at our health-care facility. I realized that undergoing this serious operation would be easier on my body after a few weeks of relaxation.

Contemplating Brain Surgery

Whether I was terrified of the outcomes of an approaching operation, the possibility of more physical pain, or the unknowns of it all, exposing the emotions these threats elicited helped me connect with my spiritual self and encounter the Love that resides deep within all of us.

Every time I connected with this deeper part of me, I experienced a peace that carried me through those difficult months. Peace and Love have a unique role in the universe, and contemplation connects us with them. What happens when we connect with our deeper self is what I, and many others, call religious experience.

The more I have helped others pray, the more astounded I have become at the power of prayer. Prayer changes us, sometimes radically. When we behold Love, we become more like the Love that we contemplate. When we participate in the mysterious process of contemplation, we not only become more like Love itself, we also see more of its supreme role in earth's ongoing Dance.

You might recall a time when you were watching a sunset or holding your newborn child and something special came over you. Sometimes watching can become gazing, and holding can become beholding. Did you trust that experience and let seconds become minutes? If so, I say to you: trust these experiences and ask to be more alert to their frequency. Untamed Love is the most powerful force in the universe and much larger than our individual experiences of it. It is also a most tender embrace that holds each person's heart, always and forever. So when we take the time to contemplate it, Love can bring a happiness and fulfillment that surpasses our wildest expectations.

2

Love

We can experience God's presence in a multitude of ways. In some of this book's stories, people encounter God in an exchange of words, emotions, or a simple and mutual presence. But there will be no exchange of words or emotions in this chapter. While I was anesthetized, God did something new with me: Love thoroughly rearranged my consciousness. As soon as I was awakened from three days of anesthesia, I saw a beyond-belief Love that held everything and everyone in awe-inspiring communion. What I saw then and still see now is my prime reason for writing this book: I must speak and write about this vast untamed Love.

"Take Me"

Since I had cleared my calendar in preparation for my hospital stay, I had a month to heal the infection, relax my spirit, and ready my body for the surgery. Dr. Joseph Clemente, my primary care physician, finally certified that I was healthy, so I arrived at the hospital in the late afternoon for an early morning operation on January 9, 1991. The night before the surgery when a friend, along with several doctors and nurses, finally left the room, my pace slowed measurably. Facing serious brain surgery alone in a sterile hospital room seemed at first quite bleak. I began to share my emotions about that sterile, solitary situation with Love.

I prayed with a few lines in an article by Bernie Siegel that had caught my attention when visiting a doctor's office. I considered two attitudes he underscored. He compared those who say "Why me?" with those who say "Try me" when confronted with perilous illness and considered the effect each can have on our health. Neither of those categories attracted me, but as I read, I noticed a subtle shift in my experience of aloneness and fear. I felt Love growing stronger within me, and soon a response that felt right emerged. From deep within me I said to God, "Take me." A mutual and intimate Love accompanied these words. God's alluring presence and my letting go blended and deepened. As I prayed, the allurement intensified and a deep peace and joy embraced me. I quickly fell asleep and slept peacefully until a nurse woke me the next morning.

When the nurses finished the preparations, I had some time to myself. I knew I might not be walking on my own after the operation, so I roamed the hallway with an intravenous pole following me at arm's length. The peace and joy I had fallen asleep with were still strong. The fear, anxiety, and sadness of the previous months were gone. By now they had lost their power—at least for this time. Nothing interfered with this freedom and joy—not an intravenous pole, a stretcher ride, or the sterility of an operating room.

When I arrived in the surgical area, Billy Martin was the first member of the medical team to greet me. As he applied the electrodes to my head, we again shared some laughs. Except for my attire and surroundings, one might have thought I was preparing for vacation, because laughter flowed easily. Letting go during the previous months had loosened me. As the medical team did the final preparations, my interior freedom surprised me. Undoubtedly this peacefulness had a positive effect on the surgery itself.

At that time, being anesthetized for three to five days was standard procedure for this surgery. Thankfully I needed only three days. During those days, I recall being semi-lucid only a few times. Two of those times were terribly scary. Immediately after the surgery, they brought me out of the anesthesia to see how I responded to questions. Once they knew I was responding appropriately, they put me to sleep again. But it took a short while before the anesthesia worked. It seemed like forever, because I felt as though I had been hit by an immense truck. May I never again experience that type of physical diminishment. At that point my physical frailty was too much to bear; I desired the escape anesthesia would provide. Even when religious experience is strong, we remain human and carry all the vulnerability that entails. In the pain and insecurity of the operation's immediate aftermath, I lost sight of God's presence.

I woke once or twice during that night. Being hooked to so many machines was terribly frightening. The respirator was especially scary, because I could not breathe on my own or talk freely. There was a nurse assigned to my own small NICU (Neurosurgical Intensive Care Unit) for the entire night. She was wonderfully reassuring. As I tried to write a question, she tried hard to answer it. Mainly her calm manner soothed my frayed nerves. Though I will never know her, I honor her and all nurses who comfort those who are very sick.

Awaking to Love's Communion

When they woke me three days later, the horrible sensation of being run over by a truck had disappeared. Soon after, a friend came to see me. I could have talked about tubes emanating from my brain and body, double vision, a deaf ear, facial paralysis, physical imbalance, zero energy, eyelids that did not shut, an utterly bedridden body, or other impairments. Instead, Love and the communion I saw were all I talked about. Waking from three days of anesthetized sleep paled before an inner awakening. While I had been unconscious, my way of seeing had changed radically. I knew instantly that a communion of Love cradles, nourishes, stirs, and dances the universe. This Dance transcended anything I had conceived or could ever conceive.

It has taken me twenty years to understand what occurred well enough to write about it. As I try to describe this new way of seeing, I know I am trying to describe the indescribable and explain the unexplainable. Compared to the experience, my words and concepts are inadequate—terribly so. I tried to tell my family, friends, community members, and students that we are all immersed within something far grander than we are. In fact, we are immersed in something that surpasses our grandest mental imaginings and our most expansive scientific theories. The fidelity and benevolence of this universal Dance astounded me.

Love Is All There Is

This radical change in consciousness was utterly simple, though difficult to explain. Once I was alert again, I saw the unifying power of Love as never before. Any dualistic thinking that I possessed before my surgery had disappeared. Earth and heaven, body and spirit, sexuality and spirituality, and so many other dichotomies had simply vanished. If there was anything left in me that placed more value on heaven over earth, spirit over body, spirituality over sexuality, man over woman, people over animals, plants, or rocks, it all vanished. Love was all I saw, and it was everywhere. It reigned supreme, and there was absolutely no superiority connected with this Love.

I had been taking my connection with Love seriously since I entered religious life. In my mid-twenties the field of spirituality began to fascinate me. By my late twenties I chose the Christian spiritual tradition as my field of study. This choice was not only a theoretical one. Throughout my twenties I developed a more experiential relationship with God. Spirituality became a field of study and an ongoing relationship with Love. By the time I prepared for my operation, I had learned some things about God. But when the doctors brought me out of anesthesia, I experienced a presence throughout this universe that could have stood what hair I had left on end.

I wrote in the introduction that I no longer see Love as one human emotion among others or even a preeminent emotion. Nor is it the sole possession of human beings. I see Love as a sacred and universal presence that holds, leavens, and enlivens everything and everyone. Divinity moves "here, there, and everywhere," making all things sacred. Love is God, and God is Love.

But Love is also a tender embrace that holds each individual heart. With each increase of Love within us, our spiritual self grows stronger. When I write about our deeper self, I am also referring to Love. Teilhard de Chardin, a Jesuit scientist and mystic who died in 1955, says, "The day will come when, after harnessing the ether, the winds, the tides, gravitation, we shall harness for God the energies of love. And on that day, for the second time in the history of the world, the human being will have discovered fire."[1] It will be a momentous evolutionary happening when human beings, as a species, rely on Love's fire in their depth.

New Center of Consciousness

You may wonder if the drugs I was given during surgery caused this mental change. Though those drugs lost their power soon after the surgery, my awareness of communion has never changed during the last twenty years. Love alone evokes such thorough and permanent conversion. Human beings experience mental transformations throughout their lives. Child psychologists tell us that very small children experience a sense of oneness with that which surrounds them. They gradually develop a sense of individuality that becomes pronounced in adolescence and young adulthood.

At the age of forty-three, I experienced another massive transformation. My awareness of communion superseded my awareness of individuality. Today my former way of seeing is a vague memory, and recalling it is as difficult as explaining my present experience of communion. After my operation, my center for seeing, knowing, and loving moved; the center point of my consciousness was no longer the individual self, and this shift changed everything. Previously, God and community meant a great deal to me, but I related with everyone through my individual self. When I looked out, I saw many individuals and their varying depths of connection with each other and me.

Now, my center was within a communion of being; this communion of Love held everyone and everything. This was no mere adjustment in perspective, as if before my surgery I focused on individuals and afterward I saw the whole. This transformation has only surface similarities to the considerations of "the one and the many" that has engaged philosophers for millennia. For me, it was a major reversal in consciousness that changed everything. Now, my consciousness and communion were one. Wherever I looked, I saw the intricate and elegant web of relationships that constitutes the universe. We are all immersed in a Love that makes us mutual and coequal companions. This new way of seeing was effortless; while I slept, Love had rearranged my mental apparatus.

This new awareness enhanced my former approach to individuality. Before my surgery I saw the universe as a gathering of individuals with the emphasis on the individuals; after it I saw the universe as a communion of individuals with the emphasis on communion. Love embraced individuality; it also enhanced its meaning. The universe's communal Dance captivated me, and I delighted in each individual aspect of creation, because I saw its deepest dimension far more clearly. Each pebble, leaf, and person was immersed in a communion of Love and glowed with exquisite interiority. We are all immersed in God's immense communion, a gathering of vitally important and infinitely unique individuals.

Being Held

This reversal highlighted the reality that I was being held more than holding. Before this experience I had focused on initiative and responsibility. For years I had experienced God's deepening Love, yet I continued to work very hard at holding everything else. Whether I focused on programs I coordinated or relationships I sustained, I was an overachiever who felt responsible for holding everything in my world together. Of course I had learned a great deal about letting go while I danced and surrendered to the Love of my life. Relating with Love often elicited in me a deepening appreciation and acceptance of surrender, but I was still a high achiever.

Then, within a few days, I moved from great achiever to utter receiver. Before surgery I had taken my body for granted, never noticing how reliably it responded to my every whim. When I awoke from surgery, my body was bedridden with no capacity for whims. For weeks I had little energy for even passive activities such as listening to music or watching television. For months others brought me food and lowered me into a whirlpool for bathing. During the early months of recovery a walker enabled me to take three fifteen-minute daily walks up and down the same short corridor. It was clear that I was being healed more than healing, being held more than holding, being danced more than dancing. Without the awareness that I was held, the physical aspect of my body's frailty would have been unbearable.

Doctors and nurses, parents and friends, all of my sisters in Mercy, along with plants, animals, and elements, formed a matrix of healing. All these forces, along with my infirm but vital efforts, gradually healed my body. This awareness of being held never left me during the recovery period. Sometimes the pain and fear or impatience and boredom that accompany a long healing process gained prominence and clouded my vision. But my awareness of communion and its profound ability to uphold the weak and the strong always returned.

A Setback

A minor but painful setback in my recovery reveals more about my experience of being held. When my body would take frightening turns, my awareness of Love's embrace would diminish. One of these scary times started with an infection.

After two weeks in the hospital I returned to McAuley Hall, the health-care center of the Sisters of Mercy. About three months after the surgery, I had gained some strength, and could finally walk without a walker for longer periods. I also began to develop an abscess in the genital area that resisted treatment. The doctor decided to drain the infection on an out-patient basis at a nearby hospital. Because the infection was worsening the night before, I was awake the entire night with significant pain. Because I was told not to eat anything after midnight, I also assumed I could not take medication.

The next morning Karen Horan, a nurse and another Sister of Mercy, drove me to the hospital. By that point I was debilitated and could not stand, let alone walk, into the hospital. Someone from the hospital came to the car, recorded the necessary information while I lay on the back seat. Then they wheeled me into the hospital preparation room, and all I could do was lie on the gurney where they placed me.

A nurse took my blood pressure as she began to prepare me. She left me immediately and called the doctor. I heard her say that my blood pressure had dropped to an alarming point. I no longer remember the exact numbers, but the doctor ordered something given intravenously that she immediately administered. I knew everyone was concerned, but it had little impact on me. I had no capacity for engagement of any type. I could manage a semblance of attention, but that was the limit of my abilities. Whatever they fed me intravenously strengthened me. By the time the doctor checked me, my blood pressure had risen, and I was alert again, so they prepared me for minor surgery. It went smoothly, but they admitted me for an overnight stay at the hospital to be sure my blood pressure had stabilized.

Almost as soon as I returned to our health-care facility, I realized I had contracted the same stomach virus that my hospital roommate had. The pain triggered by this stomach infection wreaked havoc on my weak body. It kept me awake during that night. I could only be still, endure the pain, and wait for it to subside. I was grateful for the attentiveness of Mary Price, the night nurse at our health-care facility. She knew I was in pain, and gave me the one dose of medicine allowed. It wore off within an hour. Then she sat next to my bed for the longest time. The following morning I received more medicine, and the pain diminished. The pain of the abscess, a drastic drop in blood pressure, and a painful stomach virus had depleted the energy reserves my body had gained.

During that painful time, I could not focus on the communion that was holding me. But once the pain disappeared, and I could walk again, I visited our chapel. The morning sun filtered through the stained-glass windows, splattering the softest colors around the walls and floor. Under normal circumstances, I would have knelt and prayed in the back pew. When it comes to spirituality, or anything for that matter, I dislike showiness. Still, my gratitude eclipsed self-consciousness and forced me to walk up the main aisle and kneel before the altar. I knelt in utter gratitude for doctors and nurses, medicine and immune systems, and God. They had sustained me in great weakness, so relief and gratitude overwhelmed me.

After recovering from three months of profound disability, unexpected infections, and a startling drop in blood pressure, I could no longer take this Dance for granted. Physical, intellectual, psychological, and spiritual forces were moving within and around me, and aiding all of my personal efforts toward health. And then there was Love. In the midst of great weakness and pain, Love caressed, embraced, and held me; this enfolding meant everything to me. I knelt in sheer relief that the pain was over, and with overwhelming gratitude for having been carried from sickness through pain into more health. The Cosmic Dance had held me within its communion, and kneeling at an altar was my way of expressing overwhelming thankfulness.

The Dance sustained me through many months of confinement and the sometimes frightening turns my body took. It was like the air I breathed, unobtrusive yet ever-present, life giving, and universal. I found joy in being held by the universe. From science I knew that all things are related; stars and microbes are my sisters and brothers. Still, it was one thing to know the great discoveries of our time and quite another to know from experience that God's universe was dancing me, especially when my body could no longer dance. I realized that all species, regardless of size, well-being, or accomplishment, are embraced by the same unfailing strength and tender Love. Through all of earth's near extinctions and leaps forward, God holds us with the hope and fidelity of which only divinity is capable. Love holds the entire universe, with its vast expanse of space and time, in one diverse communion of being.

Our Divine Right Mind

Other people have experiences similar to mine. As I completed this book someone recommended that I read *My Stroke of Insight* by Jill Bolte Taylor, because our experiences of severe brain trauma were similar. Taylor is the neuroanatomist connected with Harvard Medical School who experienced a severe stroke while alone in her apartment and lived to tell others about her recovery. While bleeding impaired the left side of her brain, she experienced a change in awareness similar to mine.

Her left brain had taught her to perceive herself as something solid and separate from other people. Once the bleeding in the left hemisphere of her brain released her from that restricted circuitry, her "soul was as big as the universe and frolicked with glee in a boundless sea"[2] during a disabling stroke. Her consciousness had ventured into the "peaceful bliss of my divine right mind," and she experienced oneness with the universe.[3]

Scientific and empirical studies of the human brain are providing us with more understanding of spiritual experience. Whether Taylor writes about her divine right mind or I write about our contemplative self, we are highlighting the mental apparatus that all human beings possess. Jill Bolte Taylor writes that her experience of losing her left brain functions caused her to believe that our "feeling of deep inner peace is neurological circuitry located in our right brain. . . . Knowing that I am part of the cosmic flow makes me feel innately safe and experience my life as heaven on earth."[4]

Barbara Bradley Hagerty, a journalist who wrote a book about our brain and spiritual experiences, interviewed many people from diverse backgrounds who experienced love, peace, and an overwhelming sense of union with the universe. These experiences always evoked "a radical and lasting change in their fundamental concepts of man's relation to the universe."[5] For nearly forty years I have listened to people tell me about similar experiences.

Concluding her book, Jill Bolte Taylor writes, "I must admit that Western civilization is a pretty challenging environment for my loving and peaceful right hemisphere character to live in."[6] Our Western society highly honors and rewards the "doing" left brain and either denies, criticizes, ignores, or merely tolerates the "being" right brain.[7] Biologically and culturally, we have refined our left brain with its details, schedules, analyses, judgments, seriousness, and compulsive activity, but we need the wisdom of our less familiar right brain more than ever. We must rely more on this boundary-free, mutual, creative hemisphere that experiences oneness with the universe. Because the activity of our left hemisphere and the contemplation of our right one are made to move in sync, our earthwide struggles need disciplined activity and contemplative receptivity. Without greater balance between stillness and movement—in their inner and outer manifestations—we may destroy our own species and much of earth.

Contemplating Communion

Some of us believe that our "divine right mind" merely originates from our brain's "chemical firings,"[8] and others of us are convinced that these mental dynamics involve a God who communicates with us through them. Barbara Bradley Hagerty writes that sometimes her interviewees' experiences arose from drug use or disease; other times they occurred after years of meditating; and sometimes they occurred spontaneously with no apparent catalyst. Since the universe loves diversity, disagreement about the source of these prevalent phenomena is understandable.

I encourage my readers to trust their experiences and not be overly concerned about their source; I have found that the source reveals itself in time. I do not see my awakening as special or out of the ordinary; rather I consider it to be a normal part of human growth. Thomas Berry, the visionary cultural historian who died in 2009, offers a description of the human species that places our experiences of oneness in a context that fits for me. He writes that the human species is "a mystical quality of the earth, a unifying principle, an integration of the various polarities of the material and the spiritual, the physical and the psychic, the natural and the artistic, the intuitive and the scientific. We are the unity in which all these inhere."[9]

Imagine that! For billions of years Love has evolved a species that holds within it the material, psychic, and spiritual dimensions of the entire universe. *Homo sapiens* has come so far, yet we have only begun. Global communication happens instantaneously, and life-spans lengthen rapidly, but we have so much to learn about Love. We have grown physically, emotionally, and intellectually, but, as a species, we have only begun to develop our spiritual depth—only begun to consciously connect with Love itself.

We embody the mystical quality of earth. To experience this reality we only have to connect more often with this deeper part of us, where all things are one. Have you ever sat by an utterly calm lake that elicited stillness in you? In that peace and stillness you may have sensed that everything was progressing as it should, or you may have felt a simple but profound connection with that lake and everything else. This simple experience is related to my awareness of communion, because whenever we encounter Love, we also experience something of the oneness it sustains. I invite you to be on the lookout for the deep connections that Love evokes. Love dances all of us, always; if we are awake, we experience the happiness that its communion can arouse.

Notes

1 Pierre Teilhard de Chardin, *The Heart of Matter* (New York: Harcourt, 1978), 86–87.

2 Jill Bolte Taylor, *My Stroke of Insight* (New York: Penguin, 2006), 69.

3 Ibid., 61.

4 Ibid., 168–69.

5 Barbara Bradley Hagerty, *Fingerprints of God* (New York: Riverhead Books, 2009), 130–31.

6 Taylor, *My Stroke*, 176.

7 Ibid., 169.

8 Hagerty, *Fingerprints*, 131.

9 Thomas Berry, *The Great Work* (New York: Bell Tower, 1999), 174–75.

3

Earth Spirituality

When the doctors revived me from anesthesia, I saw everything as a communion. Matter and spirit were more intimately connected than I had previously thought. Of course they were different, but in God's Love there was not even the slightest separation. Love's Cosmic Dance guided everything and everyone. Each speck and massive expanse of this universe possesses spiritual depth. As I cradle a daffodil, I delight in caressing the face of God.

Awaking to Earth's Spirituality

Two weeks after the surgery, I left the hospital and arrived at McAuley Hall, one of my community's health-care facilities. Since it is nestled in a low mountain range, I could enjoy earth's holiness, if only from the window. Whenever I sauntered down the hall with my walker, I would gaze upon winter's bare forest outside my window. I greatly appreciated this ability to contemplate nature through a window. It was more than I could do in the hospital. Because my balance, hearing, and eyesight on the right side of my body were gone, and my body was extremely weak, it took a few months before I could walk outside.

Finally an increased strength and the ability to walk unaided coincided with the arrival of spring. During April I began taking brief and slow walks outside and could finally handle face-to-face contact with earth's holiness. Each encounter with a familiar creation became a celebration of the ordinary as extraordinary.

I remember my first visit to some magnolias that surround our health-care facility. Though I had enjoyed their beauty before, I had taken them for granted. Previously these blossoms, so reliable each spring, faded in comparison with the needs of the human community. *I had never had time for magnolias!* Now, as my body forced me to slow down, I inched forward toward one group of blossoms. My pace enhanced the anticipation. A long and leisurely look enabled me to see them for the first time. Their blossoms enthralled me. On the outside, the color of the petals moved from a deep rose to the faintest pink. Inside, they were pure white. Their delicate beauty awed me.

The common is thoroughly uncommon, when we know how to see and take the time to contemplate. God holds everything and everyone with the same tenderness. Once I so clearly saw this, I could never again speak or write solely about human spirituality. Since Love resides within everything, all things possess spiritual depth. For the year and a half that followed my surgery, I stopped at every flower I met to acknowledge its holiness.

Matter and Spirit Dance

I find it terribly sad that with the dawn of science, religion and science became enemies. Religionists and scientists share equal responsibility for this divide. I cannot explain how we human beings created such irreconcilable camps, but I do know this development has nothing to do with Love. I am also grateful that these rigid boundaries are softening. The God I encounter dances science and religion, matter and spirit, earth and humanity mutually. I cannot imagine how Love could support these divides. After all, there is little room for silly divisions on a dance floor.

I do not personally recall experiencing this split between science and religion, matter and spirit. Soon after I entered religious life, I discovered *Teilhard de Chardin and the Mystery of Christ* by Christopher Mooney; reading this book and others by Teilhard helped me understand my intimacy with earth. Teilhard de Chardin's eloquent words about matter's spirituality dissolved any divisions that might have developed in me. "Crimson gleams of Matter, gliding imperceptibly into the gold of Spirit...and through all this there blows, animating it and spreading over it a fragrant balm, a zephyr of Union—and of the Feminine. The Diaphany of the Divine at the heart of a glowing Universe, as I have experienced it through contact with the Earth—the Divine radiating from the depths of blazing Matter."[1]

Then I had brain surgery, and any hint of separation in my mental categories was rearranged. When the doctors revived me from anesthesia, I saw beneath all these categorical distinctions and the hierarchies of worth they can promote. In the depths of everything I saw Love alone, and its profound ability to hold everything and everyone in communion. As spiritual insight deepens we more keenly perceive Love, and the way it enfolds all things mutually.

One month after my surgery I yearned to read scientists and mystics who understood communion. Fortunately, this yearning was accompanied by enough physical strength to read once again. Since I would be confined to bed for several months, I had plenty of time for it. Initially, the writings of John of Ruusbroec, Thomas Berry, and Brian Swimme preoccupied me. My double vision forced me to read with one eye only. As I contemplated the little I could read, it permeated my being, revealing the profound connection between matter and spirit.

John Ruusbroec was a twelfth-century Flemish mystic and a little-known genius in the Christian spiritual tradition. I was drawn to read some of his writing during the weeks before surgery. During my recovery I focused on a few pages where Ruusbroec eloquently described the Love of God and the union it engenders. For him this loving, fruitful unity is the source of everything. "Here all creatures are therefore one being and one life." This unifying embrace "is beyond time, that is, without any before or after, in an eternal flow."[2] As this eternal flow pervaded my consciousness, I saw it everywhere. Now my image of God included a cosmic flow that is also loving communion. Despite profound physical diminishment, I trusted the reality of this eternal, loving flow that held everything. It sustained me through a long recovery process.

Though a few lines from Ruusbroec supported me deeply, the evolutionary cosmologist Brian Swimme and the cultural historian Thomas Berry gave me a context for my experience and a vision of the universe. They not only situated the universe's evolution within communion but also brought deep and inclusive insight to its mystic dimension.

When I finally read their collaborative work, *The Universe Story*, I reveled in the words, "To be is to be related. Nothing is itself without everything else."[3] They use the image of an unborn grizzly bear to ground interrelatedness. As an unborn grizzly develops she is related to the outside world, even to the original "flaring forth." Throughout millions of years, the universe evolved her arm, paw, and claws, enabling her to snare her first Chinook salmon. This genetic code will trigger delight when she tastes her first blackberries. "The face of the bear, the size of her arm, the structure of her eyes, the thickness of her fur—these are dimensions of her temperate forest community. The bear herself is meaningless outside the enveloping web of relations."[4]

As I contemplated Ruusbroec, Berry, and Swimme, I also saw a seamless connection between science and spirituality, matter and spirit, and earth and humanity. Once we see everything from within the matrix of relationships, spirituality and science become equally important for the uniqueness each discipline brings to human understanding. Still, like all human endeavors to understand the whole, each field of study finds its deeper meaning through its immersion within communion. From within their shared immersion, they have meaning and interrelatedness.

Le Point Vierge

At some point after my surgery, I reread sections of *Conjectures of a Guilty Bystander* by Thomas Merton. He had another way of writing about earth spirituality and the holiness of everything. On the corner of Fourth and Walnut in Louisville, Kentucky, he had a powerful experience of oneness. As he watched many seeming strangers rushing around, he realized he loved all of them, "they were mine and I theirs."[5] Suddenly he saw "the secret beauty of their hearts, the depths of their hearts where neither sin nor desire nor self-knowledge can reach, the core of their reality, the person that each one is in God's eyes."[6]

He called this deep center of each person *le point vierge*, a French term that he found impossible to translate precisely. He said that seeing this simple and deep point in people rushing around shopping was like waking from an illusion. "If only they could see themselves as they really *are*. If only we could see each other that way all the time. There would be no more war, no more hatred, no more cruelty, no more greed. But it cannot be explained. There is no way of telling people that they are all walking around shining like the sun."[7]

Earth's *le Point Vierge*

Many of us can gaze at a parent, spouse, or child and experience a Love that takes our breath away. Likewise, we can look at magnolias and see heaven. When this happens I believe we connect with our spiritual self and also relate to the spiritual depth of the universe. Two years later Merton expanded on the idea of *le point vierge*. With exhilarating prose poetry, he describes *le point vierge* of the rising sun and its chirping birds. He makes it very clear that human beings are not the only species with which Love connects; the entire universe and its planet earth dance to spiritual music. The divine twirls and whirls within everything mutually.

Merton writes about the entire valley awaking. "At two-fifteen in the morning there are no sounds except in the monastery: the bells ring, the office begins. Outside, nothing, except perhaps a bullfrog saying, 'Om' in the creek or in the guest house pond. Some nights he is in Samadhi; there is not even 'Om.'"[8] Merton's writing draws us into this particular drama. Dawn takes center stage, and human beings enter later. At first only a bullfrog participates in this stupendous event, the beginning of another day. Then birds join the celebration.

> The first chirps of the waking day birds mark the *"point vierge"* of the dawn under a sky as yet without light, a moment of awe and inexpressible innocence, when the Father in perfect silence opens their eyes. They begin to speak to Him, not with fluent song, but with an awakening question that is their dawn state, their state at the *"point vierge."* Their condition asks if it is time for them to "be." He answers "yes." Then, they one by one wake up, and become birds. They manifest themselves as birds, beginning to sing. Presently they will be fully themselves, and will even fly.
>
> Meanwhile, the most wonderful moment of the day is that when creation in its innocence asks permission to "be" once again, as it did on the first morning that ever was.
>
> All wisdom seeks to collect and manifest itself at that blind sweet point.[9]

What an amazing portrayal of earth's spirituality! The last time you contemplated the dawn, did you catch the Father opening the birds' eyes? Could you hear them ask if it was time for them to be? Did you listen to them sing, once their Father said, "Yes"? Maybe you found delight in all of creation innocently asking for permission to "be."

I recall one sunrise I watched from the top of Blackhead, Monhegan's northeasternmost cliff. I sat in perfect stillness as our Mother asked the sun, surf, cliffs, and me for that Dance. I sat spellbound as her soft golden light inched its way up the cliffs. She held me in her sway for at least thirty minutes, or as long as it took her to complete that Dance. I lingered longer because the strength of the music held me motionless throughout its variations.

Merton calls the leader of this exquisite dynamic Father,

and I call her Mother; others might call this gliding and sliding Yahweh, Tao, or the Cosmic Dance. A diversity of names only enhances the finesse and intimacy of this heart-to-heart exchange. All of creation asks permission; Mother and Father say, "Yes." This delicate colloquy is the heart of the universe; the Dancer intones and the Dance begins. This special conversation and its movement are the spirituality of everything and everyone. When we contemplate it, all distinctions disappear. Dancer and Dance are one.

Accepting the Invitation

Because *le point vierge* is everywhere, we need only see it. In his journal, after introducing the bullfrog, birds, and their Father, Merton wrote down his initial response. "With my hair almost on end and the eyes of my soul wide open I am present, without knowing it at all, in this unspeakable paradise and I behold this secret, this wide open secret which is there for everyone, free, and no one pays attention."[10]

At Fourth and Walnut he saw the "innermost, secret heart" that rests within each person. Now this secret expands and becomes a "wide open secret" that includes everything; Merton sees paradise everywhere. When we are connected with our spiritual self, anything can draw us into this inclusive Dance. For some it is a dramatic dawn; for others it is the innocence in a child's eyes. Like Merton, when we contemplate anything, analysis and conceptualization rest, and the eyes of our soul are wide open.

But certain steps help us join the Dance. First, we need to realize that we are being asked to dance. Many of us feel deeply quieted or moved while immersed in nature, yet may not realize that we are *being drawn* by Love. Second, we need to accept that we are joining something far grander than the human species. The humility to bow and curtsy helps a great deal. The dawn birds sensed invitation from the Father, who knew far more about dancing than they. The birds had no difficulty with asking permission of their Father. With ease they bow before something and/or someone much grander than they. Much of creation moves naturally with earth's inner melody, but accepting this invitation to dance can be more difficult for human beings.

Monhegan

Sometime in the early 1980s I read about Monhegan Island, its rustic environment and rugged shoreline, in a travel magazine. Then, during brain surgery God intensified my passion for earth. Nine months later, Love gave this passion an earthy body by alluring me to the island for a two-day visit. From the moment I arrived on Monhegan's wharf, I knew that this small island off mid-coast Maine was one expression of God's body. Since then I have returned every year. When an opportunity for a sabbatical arose in 1997, I lived there for six months. Then, while writing most of this manuscript, I lived on the island for four and a half months each year, so I could write about spirituality and earth.

Love's presence within this amazing ecosystem not only integrated my passions for God and earth but also reoriented my life. On Monhegan I photographed a young woman dancing to the setting sun, a father and small son gazing quietly at glistening sea glass, a muddy boy cavorting on the beach, and a tall, muscular man adoring a baby girl dwarfed in his arms. They seemed to be one with the setting sun, glistening glass, muddy beach, and tiny baby. I had no doubt they were mesmerized by these life-giving happenings. Their quiet or uproarious dancing was a response to earth's deepest movement.

Whether or not they knew it, they had asked permission to "be," and earth had responded, "Yes." I believe these people connected with the God who draws everything and everyone into a unified whole. Whether *le point vierge* is moving within human beings or throughout the universe, it is the same dynamic. Because Love holds human beings and the entire universe mutually, human beings, earth, and the cosmos are spiritual; God's embrace makes matter and spirit one.

Playing, Praying, and Dancing

People come to Monhegan for different reasons. Some come to "get away" and relax. Others come to appreciate the island's artistic tradition with its studios, galleries, and annual summer museum show. Because most of the island is left in its wild state, many come to enjoy Monhegan's untamed beauty. Some say they come because of the island's spirituality. I come here for all of these reasons. In addition, this place provides me with the solitude I need to write contemplatively and a pace I need to maintain the health I still have. Primarily, though, I return to Monhegan because here Love dances me in a special way. Here communion is flesh and blood, rock and surf, soil and plant. This dear island always reminds me of my immersion within a deeper and grander reality. Contemplating Love as it moves amid Monhegan reveals the island's spiritual depth to me.

As my intimacy with Monhegan Island deepens, I recall some advice Rachel Carson offered about writing. This famous ecologist loved the sea, especially the Maine coast. She was a highly gifted writer and scientist who in 1962 awakened the world to our destruction of earth through her book *Silent Spring*. Carson said that the discipline of writing entails being still and listening to see what your subject wants to tell you: "The initial task is to come to know our subject intimately, to understand its every aspect, to let it fill our minds. Then at some turning point, the subject takes command and the true art of creation begins."[11]

There are moments when Monhegan takes command. This occurred on a kayak trip around the island. I had first realized that kayaking thrilled me on a still river no deeper than three feet. I had been giving a day of prayer at Still Waters, a small spirituality center, in Carlisle, Pennsylvania. The kayaks in the boathouse beckoned to my adventurous spirit, and I thoroughly enjoyed my relaxed kayaking on that sunny spring day.

Once I had my own kayak, someone slowly, very slowly, followed me around Monhegan in a motorboat on a perfectly calm sea. My second trip around Monhegan was a solo trip and kayaking of another sort. I wanted to contemplate the island's massive headlands from sea level. As I began my circumnavigation, the harbor was utterly calm, as was the northern shore. The ocean and I relaxed and enjoyed our slow dancing. As I neared the northeasternmost point and rounded Blackhead, one of the highest cliffs, the sea's mood changed. Swells grew and the ocean's powerful energy pressured my kayak from opposing directions. Sightseeing ended; fast dancing began. Even a glance at Blackhead, my most beloved spot on the island, seemed foolhardy. The sea's slightest movement not only focused my mind, but engaged every fiber of my being. The kayak and I danced to the island's music and, once more, its grandeur humbled me. Then, as I passed Blackhead, the water calmed a little and I could contemplate some coves and cliffs, but only briefly, because the sea still led this Dance. As I rounded the southern shore of the island, the sea loosened its grip, and I finally relaxed. We returned to slow dancing. I could again lead the Dance and enjoy the people on the shore contemplating me. I understood their contemplation, for I had watched lone kayakers from the same vantage point. A tiny kayak on an endless ocean mesmerizes onlookers and defies understanding. Earth's mystery often humbles us.

That was my last kayak trip around the island. In the days that followed it, my body let me know that I no longer have the strength for such adventure. Now I connect with the ocean's moods by kayaking around the island's small harbor when it is utterly calm. Every time I sit in my kayak and am immersed in the sea, I experience intimacy with everything and the God who is the Cosmic Dance. This is contemplation, and it always draws me into earth spirituality.

While nature flows freely with this sacred music, human beings sometimes plod rather than dance. God moves unhindered through any part of nature, so nature can help us pray. Sometimes nature frees us of our preoccupations within minutes. Suddenly a wild bird or a tame garden can simplify our thoughts and center our mind in Love. In the two preceding chapters I asked you to trust your experiences of Love, to be on the lookout for more, and to develop a mindful practice. Here I encourage you to make presence to earth a part of your contemplative practice. Recall a time when you experienced intimacy with earth. You do not need a kayak or Monhegan Island. Maybe you were walking in a wooded glen, watching birds at a feeder, or tending your garden when you sensed that matter and spirit are held as one. Like the birds saying "yes" to their Father and Mother, did you accept Love's invitation to wake up and sing?

Notes

1 Pierre Teilhard de Chardin, *The Heart of Matter* (New York: Harcourt Brace, 1978), 16.

2 John Ruusbroec, *The Spiritual Espousals and Other Works*, trans. J. Wiseman, Classics of Western Spirituality (New York: Paulist Press, 1985), 163.

3 Thomas Berry and Brian Swimme, *The Universe Story* (New York: Harper Collins, 1992), 77.

4 Ibid., 77–78.

5 Thomas Merton, *Conjectures of a Guilty Bystander* (New York: Doubleday, 1966), 158.

6 Ibid.

7 Ibid., 157–58.

8 Ibid. 131.

9 Ibid.

10 Thomas Merton, *The Intimate Merton*, ed. Patrick Hart and Jonathan Montaldo (San Francisco: Harper San Francisco, 1999), 157.

11 Paul Brooks, *Rachel Carson: The Writer at Work* (San Francisco: Sierra Club Books, 1989), 3–4.

4

Contemplative Moments

Contemplation is an innate and under-utilized gift. Sunlight on tall grass, a child's flickering smile, or two people dancing as one can foster reveries. These moments of absorption and encounter are crucial to human happiness and the well-being of earth itself.

This rumination has more to do with attention to life than with techniques for prayer. When we ponder life carefully, we experience its deeper dimensions. Just as a baby absorbs Love from a parent holding it, when we contemplate anything, we experience a Love that holds everything. We swim in a sea of Love, and contemplation intensifies our awareness and experience of God. Moments of self-forgetfulness, receptivity, and mindfulness aid us in our connection with God.

Wildly Free Dancing

Photographing children on Monhegan became a delightful break from writing. When I needed a break during July and August, I would go to Swim Beach, where I found children covered with mud as they tried to dam small streams or exhilarated from dashing in and out of the island's icy water. One day I spotted a two-year-old child on his father's shoulders. The child's navy dungarees, mellow-yellow shirt, and red hat caught my attention. The father soon removed his son's sneakers and dungarees and his own shoes, and they both began to play at the water's edge.

Initially, I photographed them from a distance. When the

father passed me, I asked if he minded me photographing from a closer range. He seemed delighted and said, "Sure, but use my camera, too." The constant motion of children is a photographic challenge, but they were enjoying their party by the sea, and I quickly joined their fun.

Before long, the father had undressed his son, and I was taking my first nude photographs. Through his lens and mine, I contemplated the freedom of their play and the joy of their Love. From one perspective, I was taking photographs; from a deeper angle, I was dancing. My mind had moved from the seriousness of writing to the frivolity of playing in mud. One photo reminds me of a delightful moment. The child was wearing his father's hat and sunglasses. As he looked out at the ocean, the pleasure of sheer fun and a nude body brought a magnificent smile to his face. It was as if he said, "Here I am, world, aren't I grand!"

This was contemplation at its best. Father and son, camera and I let go and danced. Whenever I behold that child's smile and his unselfconscious pride, I see Love, the spiritual dimension of everything and everyone. We swim in a sea of Love, and contemplation enables us to dance to its melody. But here is the clincher: contemplation is more about letting go and dancing than about planning, working, and building. The first three chapters highlighted our immersion in a communion of Love. Now I stress that in order to pray, we need to forget ourselves and recognize that which surrounds and holds us.

Contemplation is a simple mental process that intensifies Love, strengthens relationships, and elicits celebration. That father, son, and I were utterly unselfconscious as we reveled in an ocean of Love. This type of gazing is more like a happening than an accomplishment. During our meditative moments Love assumes control and gives us what we most need. But if we avoid these happenings, something dies inside us. Gazing at an ocean, playing in mud, and touching the hand of another sustain us. Without contemplation and the depth of connection we experience through it, life is bland, and we plod rather than dance through it, because we miss the glory that surrounds us.

Giving and Receiving Love Takes Time

Many of us experience contemplative moments when we are immersed in nature or beholding someone we love. Our minds can shift from conceptual thought to contemplative gazing in an instant. Unique lighting on a landscape, the smile of someone we love, or the freedom of playing in mud can instantly move us from conceptualization to contemplation.

How do I define contemplation? *Webster's* says contemplation entails viewing something or someone "with considered attention." Though this entire book describes this art form, I start by saying it is a long and loving look at anything or anyone. This type of gazing connects us to our own depth, where we encounter a Love that creates and enlivens human Love. God is the source of all human Love, but God's Love is stronger and more unconditional than our best experiences of this human emotion. Essentially, contemplation is an encounter that intensifies our experience of and transformation into Love. Any increase of Love is spiritual growth, and the reverse is also true.

But finding the balance between contemplation and action is difficult for all of us. Pondering anything evokes a receptive rather than an achievement-oriented attitude. Without question, our human orientation toward completing tasks and fulfilling responsibilities is crucial to earth's continuance. But poets and prophets tell us that incessant activity destroys the spirit.

Anyone who has read even a few of Mary Oliver's poems immediately senses her meditative spirit. In her brief but penetrating poem "Going to Walden," she highlights a destructive aspect of excessive activity: "How dull we grow from hurrying here and there."[1] The poem is filled with irony because it revolves around a decision to forgo a visit to Walden Pond, an American symbol for quiet reflection. The poem underscores how easily and subtly the appeal of activity can sabotage our ability to receive Love.

When we lose our connection with our deeper self, our encounters with the Love that sustains us become dull at best and nonexistent at worst. Thomas Merton named our fetish for action as our greatest crisis; through it we have lost our sense of contemplation. His insight is even more applicable to our time than his: "The greatest menace to our capacity for contemplation is the incessant fabrication of tawdry, empty stimuli which kill the receptivity of the soul."[2]

Few of us are called to become a Trappist. Still, I believe the survival of the human species and the health of our earthly home depend on our ability to integrate contemplation and activity. In his book *Ritalin Nation*, Richard DeGrandpre says, "Leisure, slowness, idleness, relaxation, simplicity—these all have become pastimes of American culture, replaced by an almost singular obsession with speed."[3] If as a society we continue to canonize the gross domestic product and the level of activity our economy requires of too many, we will not only diminish our spirits, but as DeGrandpre argues, we will also destroy the minds of our children. If too many of us maintain our rapid-fire pace, we will not only become dull but will also destroy our capacity to give and receive Love. The receptivity that contemplation fosters prevents us from seeing others as cogs in the wheels of progress and enables us to see them as creatures who, in Merton's words, "shine like the sun."

Becoming a "Servant of Another's Contemplation"

But contemplation entails more than decreasing stimuli and taking time to relax; contemplating Love involves attentiveness and expectancy. While reading an article about spiritual direction when I was twenty-six, I met someone who was attentive to and fascinated by God. Whether William Connolly was praying, offering spiritual direction, or writing, he was mindful of God's presence. I had been receiving spiritual direction and studying spirituality for some time, but at that point I read "Helping a Person Notice and Share with the Lord Key Interior Facts," an article that later became a chapter in a book.[4] That I can still remember the couch on which I read it and the light that filtered through the windows emphasizes the impact of this article on my life.

William Connolly wrote about prayer in such an experiential and relational way that I connected with him immediately. What was happening in prayer was essential to him; he was not focused on why or even how it was happening. Primarily Connolly focused on the movement of God in a particular life experience. As I read, I caught, in my own immature way, that he had a profound ability to "notice interior facts" and evoke them in those he listened to.

While reading this article and others by him, I sensed a strong attraction to offer spiritual direction to others and felt drawn to this author's approach to such direction. In the early 1980s I was accepted into the joint program in spirituality and spiritual direction at the Center for Religious Development and the Weston Jesuit School of Theology in Cambridge, Massachusetts.

On any given day at the Center for Religious Development, we would guide the prayer of, for example, a housewife from Somerville, a professor from MIT, a justice coordinator working for the Boston Archdiocese, a United Church of Christ seminary student, or a nun on sabbatical from Tanzania. The guidance we received in our individual and group supervision sessions helped us discern varied experiences of God in this diverse population. This education profoundly expanded my ability to contemplate Love's movement among all of us.

More than thirty years later I still recall Bill Connolly's innate gift for evoking our spiritual self. He was attracted to and absorbed by Love's movement. God's presence in another hooked him, and his attention became riveted on the movement of God that he heard within the directee, and all of Bill's responses further evoked this movement. He often became the "servant of another's contemplation," a phrase he would use in his teaching and later wrote about in *The Practice of Spiritual Direction*.

Because I already desired to be the servant of another's contemplation without even knowing it, this phrase focused me. As I observed Bill supporting another's contemplation, I wanted this Dance to absorb my attention as deeply as it absorbed his.

Then one day it began to happen: my attention also became riveted on what was happening, not on how or why it was happening. A middle-aged, very stressed businessman had come to me several times for spiritual direction. I had listened to his anxieties about his job and to his desire to pray. He often tried to tell Jesus about his stress but always said he felt like he was talking to a wall.[5]

But this time was different. Joe had decided to eat his lunch in a nearby park so he could get away from his job's tension and try to pray a little. When he came to our next session he started by saying, "Jesus surprised me." On a beautiful autumn day while he asked Jesus to relieve his anxiety, he suddenly sensed Jesus listening intently while sitting on the other side of the park bench. Joe said Jesus' listening relaxed him. As he walked back to the office his troubles had lifted, and his shoulders had loosened.

Because this awareness of Jesus was new for Joe, I felt relieved and glad. I asked him if he wanted to look at Jesus' presence more carefully; he seemed eager to do so. I asked if he remembered anything more about Jesus sitting on the other side of the bench. As his conversation slowed he said, "I forgot something important. When I asked for some relief, he gave me a small basket with balls in it. He asked me to look at each one as a particular concern, and then throw it to him. With each one that he caught, I felt lighter inside."

JANICE: As Jesus caught each ball and you felt lighter, did you notice anything about him?

JOE: Oh yeah, he was smiling.

JANICE: He smiled—can you say anything more about his smile?

JOE: I could tell he cared about me and wanted to help me with the stress. Imagine that—he cared enough to help me with my worries. I didn't know he could do that or would even want to do it.

JANICE: He really does care for you.

JOE: As I walked back to the office, he asked if he could stay with me for a while in the office. Though I was stunned by his question, I said, "Sure." I almost forgot this question of his. Thanks for helping me look longer at Jesus. He really does care about me. Wow!

Though our conversation was longer, this part reveals enough. As he paid attention to Jesus, Joe recalled and noticed more about his own relief and Jesus' smile and care. The simplicity of contemplation sometimes makes it seem difficult. Whether we behold Love moving in nature, in someone we love, or in a directee, attention not analysis is needed when we pray. We are surrounded by a Love that wants to be perceived. Our mindfulness helps us apprehend God's revelation.

In addition to being alert, Bill Connolly possessed an exceptional curiosity about and anticipation of God's presence. This enhanced his ability to spot Love's movement quickly in another. As I contemplated his work with others, my curiosity and anticipation intensified. As I listened to Joe say, "Jesus surprised me," and "He smiled," I felt a powerful attraction to hear more about that surprise and the smile.

Contemplating Love is a simple yet transformative process. I carefully observed Bill Connolly's work with other people; then one day I stopped trying to understand and simply began to observe and evoke God's movement in another, as on the day that Joe looked more carefully at Jesus and experienced a caring smile. Love had filled both of us with some of Bill Connolly's mindfulness, curiosity, and expectation. Love was beginning to change me into the servant of another's contemplation. Contemplating Love changes us and can help us develop a contemplative attitude toward our entire life.

Contemplating Love Everywhere

Many of us find action easy; it's prayer that's difficult. Yet we are wired for contemplation. As a spiritual director, I have witnessed many contemplative experiences. As contemplation begins and deepens, I observe people's eyes either close or cease to focus on anything in particular. Emotions are stilled or aroused, depending on the impact of inner experiences. As meditation deepens, I see bodies become quiet and eventually motionless. Sometimes a hand remains suspended in midair for twenty minutes; a person's attention is so deeply focused that he never notices this awkward position.

In *Fingerprints of God*, Barbara Hagerty introduces us to Robert Cloninger, a psychiatrist at Washington University Medical School in St. Louis. Cloninger had developed a personality test that measures our inclinations toward spirituality. His years of studying people's spiritual inclinations made him realize that there was a missing piece in his research: the soul.

> "I had to move to recognizing that we actually do have a psyche, a soul, and that it does have characteristics, and those characteristics differ from one to another."
>
> "You seem to be saying," I said carefully, "that there's nature, nurture, and then something . . ."
>
> "Mystical?" Cloninger laughed as he finished my sentence. "There is. And it's real. We really have a soul. And we really can listen to it. And it's good and it's intelligent and it's what makes life worthwhile."[6]

Cloninger is onto something, but I prefer the word "contemplative" to "mystical" and the words "deeper self" to "soul" because they seem more natural, more human. If you want to listen to the real part of you of which Cloninger speaks, be on the lookout for everyday events that hold your attention and elicit quietude. If you enjoy listening to music or relaxing with your young child, let these experiences foster your prayer. Let go of your need to do something, your drive to make sense of a difficulty, or your compulsion to control your surroundings. Behold different parts of nature or people—just behold them without analysis. There is no need to evaluate your experience, simply be present to your surroundings. Patience is crucial, because we cannot control contemplation. The more unselfconscious, receptive, attentive, and expectant you become, the easier it is to experience Love's presence everywhere and in our own depth.

We have an innate ability to gaze upon anything, and this capability can intensify our awareness of infinite and unconditional Love. While we are contemplating anything, Love sweeps us into its Dance, sometimes for a few seconds and at other times for a longer period. When the mind becomes deeply focused, it joins the depth of the universe. Feeling this Cosmic Dance in every fiber of our being is exhilarating and deeply fulfilling. We are all distinct, yet one, in this spiraling Dance. We are wired to contemplate everything, and developing a contemplative attitude toward life can make us wildly free lovers.

Notes

1 Mary Oliver, *New and Selected Poems* (Boston: Beacon Press, 1992), 239.

2 Thomas Merton, *A Search for Solitude* (San Francisco: Harper San Francisco, 1997), 102.

3 Richard DeGrandpre, *Ritalin Nation* (New York: W. W. Norton, 1999), 16.

4 William Barry and William J. Connolly, *The Practice of Spiritual Direction* (New York: Seabury Press, 1982), 65–79.

5 Whenever I write about the experiences of directees or supervisees, I have always received their permission to do so. Though the experiences are similar to those that were shared with me, I have often altered peoples' ages, locations, and backgrounds to conceal their identities.

6 Barbara Bradley Hagerty, *Fingerprints of God* (New York: Riverhead Books, 2009), 102.

5

Contemplating Everything

Contemplation can be a look, an encounter, and a relationship. Chapter 4 focused on contemplative experiences that occur spontaneously and frequently in our lives. In this chapter I consider what happens when we develop a prayerful practice that enables us to contemplate all of life. We observe Mike, a young priest, and me as we move from contemplative moments to contemplating life. Becoming contemplative not only intensifies our Love, it also makes us more familiar with God's ways.

Mike's Early Contemplation of Life

I had been offering spiritual guidance for five years, when something occurred that underscored the difference between contemplative moments and becoming contemplative. Then I had the privilege of working with several young priests in different parts of the country. Two of them had fallen in love and were struggling fiercely with mutually exclusive calls to celibacy and marriage. They wanted to remain Roman Catholic priests and to continue their deepening emotional relationships with these women. For now, this is impossible in the Roman Catholic tradition.

I met one of them, let us call him Mike, on a week-long silent retreat. When the retreat began, he said that, by the end of the retreat, he had to make a decision between celibacy and a woman he loved. He wanted to marry Carol but was not sure that this was all right with God. He was in his late twenties, and I had no idea how gifted he was at praying and discerning, let alone making decisions through these processes. It is very difficult to use discernment for decision making when we have a limited understanding of the interior movements that occur while praying.

I soon realized that using discernment to make a decision by the end of the week was impossible. Mike had little ability to notice the presence of God in his prayer, let alone to discern between God's presence and other inner dynamics. He had started to fall in love with Carol the year before he was ordained. No one had slowed his ordination process or given him any spiritual guidance to deal with what was happening. So he was ordained, and the dual attractions to marriage and the priesthood only intensified.

During his retreat he placed more trust in God's responses to his prayer. Gradually he gained some ability to recognize interior movements that signaled God's presence. As he walked along the ocean on the last day of the retreat, Mike sensed God's personal Love for the first time. He experienced Jesus walking with him along the water's edge, loving him like a brother during the entire walk. Since Mike could not remember any interpersonal communication with Jesus before the retreat, much less Jesus' Love, this was a powerful experience for him.

For a short time they chatted about life's details, and Mike finally gained the courage to share his fierce struggle with Jesus. As we talked later about this experience, Mike said Jesus asked him to stay in the priesthood. If Jesus loved him that much, he wanted to do what Jesus asked, so he promised he would let go of his relationship with Carol. Given the circumstances of Mike's youth, his early attempt at experiential prayer, and his confusion about his dilemma, this response did not sound like Jesus to me. I trusted the Love, but the comment about celibacy seemed more hollow than genuine to me.

Since we were closing the retreat, and Mike wavered in his decision, I asked him if he would be interested in continuing his discernment through monthly direction sessions. He agreed.

When we connected several weeks later, Mike said that he had not been able to let go of Carol. It was almost as if he had forgotten the experience on the beach. I was not surprised and was even glad, since it was not clear what Jesus wanted for this young man. Mike and I saw each other regularly for another year and a half. During that time his relationship with Jesus deepened. Simultaneously he was more able to distinguish between Jesus' presence and other influences in his prayer.

Mike gradually let go of some of his projections onto Jesus and met the real Jesus. He was dumbfounded to realize that Jesus appreciated and even enjoyed his relationship with Carol. Gradually Mike realized that he was projecting his mother's desire that he be a priest onto Jesus. As soon as he could separate his mother's desires from those of Jesus, he realized Jesus was calling him to marry Carol. Mike eventually left the priesthood and married her.

Since then I have listened to the discernments of many celibate people. Some of those who doubt their call to celibacy realize that God wants them to remain celibate, and with God's help they do so. Others like Mike realize that God is drawing them into a committed spousal relationship, and they let go of the Roman Catholic priesthood or religious life. Like Mike, they gradually realize they misunderstood the call to celibacy. Love is so often different from our expectations of it; it is through deep and prolonged listening that we best hear Love's genuine voice. Contemplating Love heightens our awareness of its ways.

Discerning Experiences and Relationships

Mike's is a classic situation that Ignatius of Loyola responds to in one of his rules for discernment. He invites spiritual directors to pay close attention to "the beginning, middle, and end" of a discernment.[1] Since God's ways are not always our ways, paying attention to every point in the discernment is crucial.

I have been discerning God's ways for nearly fifty years. The longer I observe them, the subtler they become. When I am discerning serious decisions, I need all the help I can get.

Discerning Love's movement in the world, and in our own hearts, is often a challenge. In Mike's case, we see that discernment takes time, especially in life-changing situations. We are on more secure ground when we take time and seek help with significant decisions, especially when a great deal of emotion is involved.

As a species we have only begun to perceive the ways of Love; in this area we are still slow learners. I hope this story illustrates that individual spiritual experiences are not as fulfilling or sustaining as an ongoing relationship with our spiritual self and the Love that resides there. It was Mike's year-and-a-half relationship with Jesus that led him into a life-giving decision. Gazing at Love for a while heightened his awareness of Love's ways. Mike was surprised that God wanted him to follow his deep desire to love and marry Carol. More important, Mike realized God desired this because it would make Mike happy, and Love wanted him to be happy. Mike and I had to let go of our direction relationship when I moved too far from him, so I know nothing more about his story. I do know that Mike began to contemplate Love and its ways. Contemplative moments happen spontaneously, but contemplating life changes us as it intensifies our Love.

My Initial Steps in a Relationship with God

I had experienced a great deal of confusion and pain in my senior year of high school, while I considered whether I would enter religious life. Letting go of a boyfriend I dated steadily and leaving family and friends for a life that was quite different from anything I knew elicited turmoil. When I let Love draw me, I had a deep sense of rightness, even when the rest of my life was upsetting. When I ignored or fought this inner attraction, everything went awry. While I had no knowledge of or experience with dynamics like these, somehow I sensed this allurement as God's way of communicating with me. Whether I liked it or not, Love was calling me to religious life. It gripped my heart, brought me through the turmoil of my senior year and into religious life. This alluring force and its attraction were the beginning of my conscious relationship with God. Love's strong and persistent hold on me revealed its desire that I experience a relationship with, not simply an experience, of it. This relationship gradually intensified my understanding of Love's ways.

I enjoyed the fifteen women with whom I entered, our first year of college courses, and connections with lay students in those classes. I disliked the many rules, structured days, and traditional approach to religious life, but studies and friends helped me accept the things I found hard. At some point during that year I realized that entering religious life must have been the right decision because an interior peace predominated. During the six months before I entered, I had sometimes cried myself to sleep. Leaving family and friends was difficult, especially when I was not sure I liked this idea. Now my crying had ceased.

I shifted, however, from peace to turmoil during the second year, my first novitiate year. In 1965 Vatican II, an ecumenical council of the Roman Catholic Church, called women religious to renew themselves so as to respond to the needs of the modern world. Our formation directors responded valiantly to the church's call, but our formation program was still quite traditional. Hindsight tells me that our group entered with a different mind-set than some of the groups that preceded us. We challenged the traditions, and those who followed us were even more challenging. Being young and inexperienced, we had no clarity of vision, but the ferment already happening among professed sisters enlivened us.

The church sets aside the canonical year as a special time in religious life. During this phase the young women in training devote more time to spiritual growth and a more intense study of religious life itself. That year we had none of the academic study that I enjoyed and more of the housework that I disliked. Now there was nothing to distract me from the rules and schedules that I had a hard time relating to.

Many a day I looked down our hill to Route 22 far below and begged God to loosen his grip so I could leave. Sometimes I pleaded, other times I ranted and raved. I never shared this revolt with superiors; if I left religious life, I wanted it to be my choice. I also tried bargaining with God. I requested just a few more years to date and see the world. I was utterly sincere as I prayerfully asked for a few years; I promised to return at some point. By the end of our first two years, five of my companions had left religious life; I longed to follow them down the hill. Late at night that year I hid in the tub room reading William Golding's *Lord of the Flies*. I hated the brutal parts of that book, but it was the closest I could get to a little wildness. Things were way too tame and controlled for me in that novitiate year.

But God never let go of me. His attraction has always surpassed my resistance. Even as I complained or begged for more adventurous and forward-looking experiences, I could feel God holding my heart and tethering it to religious life. I use the word "tether" purposely because despite my inner resistance to that time in the novitiate, I felt like God had shackled my heart to religious life. No matter how hard I tried to free myself, God's grip on my heart was always stronger.

Through all of my kicking and screaming, I grew a great deal. As I look back from my present vantage point, I see that revolt as part of my earliest growth in relationship with Love. I learned a great deal about God, prayer, and myself. What happened between God and me that year was anything but peaceful, and certainly not graceful. Through my raving and ranting, God stayed close. I would sense God's Love for me and everyone else whenever I read Teilhard or a few other books that I asked my father to get for me on the sly. I did not sense Love's closeness when I bargained or wrestled. Then I was too focused on myself to see anything but my needs and wants. Yet when I pleaded and fought, I sensed someone was listening, though that sense was vague at best.

But when I tired of my complaints or walked amid the nature that surrounded us, I quieted. Then I felt God's warmth and compassion flow through me. He seemed to understand my confusion and anger far more than I did. His acceptance helped me realize that I could bring anger, fear, pain, and joy to God. Love not only stayed close as I raved and ranted; Love responded to me throughout that year whenever I left enough room for it to enter. I did not get the expansive adventures for which I asked. God knew that seeing the world was not what I really wanted. A prayer of Julian of Norwich, a fourteenth-century English mystic, highlights the part of our humanity that was so active in me that year. "God in your goodness give me yourself, for you are enough for me. . . . And if I ask for anything which is less, always I am in want."[2] We can be so unaware of, ambivalent about, and resistant to the one thing that matters a great deal in life. Whenever I mistook anything for the deepest Love, I was utterly restless and unfulfilled.

In addition to discovering that God stayed very close while I shared my messiest emotions and restlessness, I glimpsed another aspect of prayer. I began to realize that the more honest I was with myself and God, and the longer I waited for God's response, the more deeply God would respond to me. I remember a particular time when I was preoccupied with whether I should stay or leave religious life. Finally one night as I stood longingly looking down at the lights on Route 22, I heard God say, "You want Love, not lights." As Love flooded my heart and filled my body, my confusion about religious life eased at least for a while.

This was only a beginning; it took much longer for me to develop a steady and evolving openness to God's desires. Being able to express my deeper feelings to God, no matter how messy, has grown over the years, but my transparency with close friends and God began at that point.

Having the vulnerable parts of my life embraced in an unconditional loving way has only elicited more Love and openness on my part toward God. This was the earliest development of mutuality between God and me. As I remember how God embraced my resistance and vulnerability then and has held me ever since, I recall Julian's description of eternal Love. She says that "he who is highest and mightiest, noblest and most honourable, is lowest and humblest, most familiar and courteous."[3]

I now know this Love has been with me through all the ups and downs of my life. Contemplating everything and everyone entails loving and leisurely looks at weakness as well as strength.

As God relates more familiarly with us, we cease to experience him as distant and superior. We gradually find a familiar, courteous, and close Love. Mike found a God who knew marrying Carol would bring him deep happiness, and God desired that for him. Love knew that religious life would bring me deep joy and tethered my heart to its post even as I resisted his embrace. Relating mutually with Love has brought a meaning to my life that I could never have imagined at nineteen. Gradually Love heightened Mike's and my awareness of its ways.

Contemplation Becomes Simpler

While offering spiritual direction to others, I always witness a simplification of their prayer. Many of us can miss this dynamic. But if people faithfully develop their spirituality, it will simplify. Though I have often seen this in the prayer of others, it is much easier to use my own experience when describing a forty-year-long simplification.

I just considered how prayer developed in my early twenties. Then in my late twenties a shift occurred when I began to think less and contemplate more during prayer. As I told God what was happening in my life or reflected on a spiritual book I was reading, I would move from one thought or emotion to another, and somewhere amid my thoughts and emotions I sometimes sensed God's presence. I was always more relaxed when immersed in nature; there I more easily sensed Love's embrace.

But later, on one of my retreats, this effortful and complex dynamic of thoughts, emotions, and connections suddenly simplified. My powers of analysis were turned off, and my emotions were quieted, but only while I prayed. It literally seemed as if someone had reached inside my head and jammed these frequencies. I had made several retreats at the Jesuit Center for Spiritual Growth in Wernersville, Pennsylvania, and loved to pray while walking outside. The center has miles of wooded fields and forest paths that elicit prayer. But this shift in my brain even affected my ability to walk while praying. I vividly recall my first experience of this mental quieting, because I had to stop walking and sit still under a tree. Because I liked to walk, I expressed my annoyance with God.

This transformation is embedded in my brain because it was so abrupt, pronounced, and uncontrollable. I thought I had lost my ability to pray, so I anxiously complained to my retreat director, who encouraged me to trust this quieting, because she sensed God in it. Since I had visited her for guidance with my prayer on a monthly basis for several years, I trusted her wisdom about God's ways with me. For the rest of that retreat I would sit on the benches outside. Even though the stillness felt awkward and thoughts and emotions plagued my prayer and distracted me from the stillness, I tried to accept the inner stillness I experienced.

The simplification of my prayer continued, and amid the ups and downs of my life my director helped me trust it. Since I had lost my ability to pray in a more mentally active manner, acceptance was really my only choice. It took two or three years before I could relax with, appreciate, and accept the intimacy of this quieter prayer. I could no longer work at prayer or influence what I thought and felt during it. Now Love had more control and moved more freely within me when I contemplated everything.

Gradually I came to love this quieter prayer. During my thirties prayer simplified even more. Sometimes I experienced a gentle movement of Love and peace. At other times, I sensed loving stillness; God and I were simply present to each other. I knew God was the movement and the stillness. I cherished our quiet time as Love moved between and around our hearts; our intimacy brought deep joy to my life. The more I contemplated Love, the more I learned about its ways. God desired to love me and be loved in return. What I was doing and accomplishing never seemed to matter as much as this simple, intimate, and deep exchange of Love. I felt God's Love in my heart, and its simple depth stilled my entire body. I eventually became so comfortable with it that it would last for as long as we prayed, and I often found it hard to let go of this closeness.

Contemplation Becomes Communion

Then when I was forty-three I awoke from my surgery with another radical simplification. The first change had affected the way I prayed; this second one affected consciousness itself. The center of my consciousness had shifted, but it took a while before I had this much clarity. When I awoke from the anesthesia, I immediately saw everything differently. There was no longer an interpersonal awareness when I prayed, only loving communion. Even the slightest distinction between an "I" and a "thou" was gone. Before, differentiation had predominated in my consciousness; now, communion prevailed. Everything and everyone, including me, was held so intimately by Love that distinctions no longer mattered.

After my surgery loving communion was so intimate, precious, and all-pervasive that I did not miss the interpersonal intimacy I had experienced over the years. When this new Love caught my attention, I experienced an ecstasy that often overwhelmed me; I would cry from joy over a flower, a nurse's kindness, or the repeated realization that I was alive. Since the profound physical disability of brain surgery was entirely new to me, I now assume that this euphoria was God's unexpected and personal gift to me. Significant disability was easier to accept while my spirit soared.

Now I also see this elation as my psyche's adjustment to my new way of seeing. In previous chapters I emphasized that my new vision was beyond anything I could have imagined of Love. From my depth I knew that Love held everything and everyone unconditionally and forever. From one perspective, profound joy was the only appropriate response to such brilliance.

It took some time for the rest of my being to adjust to this new way of seeing. It took even longer to gain the clarity necessary to write about it. These joyful eruptions gradually quieted, as my whole being assimilated this reality. Then I had to deal with the diminishment of my previous "I-Thou" awareness. Before my surgery, prayer had been simple and quiet. Now it was exceedingly simple and quiet. Sometimes this stillness was disorienting, and I would again fear I was not praying at all.

Even the simplest internal flow of Love that I experienced before my surgery was gone. Love was present in all of its beauty, but communion was simple, still, and utterly beyond my control. When I doubted my experience, God would quietly reassure me, and an inner peace would replace the doubt.

What happened to my awareness of individuality was and still is amazing. Awareness of individuality has given way to greater unselfconsciousness. At some point during my three days of anesthesia, a softening occurred between me and the "not me" that makes up the rest of the universe. When I pray and simply live, individuality is of no consequence; Love is all that matters. My experience of Love can be so terribly simple that I am often unaware of its movement in the way I was before my surgery. Depending on the anxieties of my life and the suffering they cause, I may lose sight of this reality for a time, but its truth is never far away, and awareness of Love's fidelity soon returns. Prayer reassures me that the cosmos and I are faithfully held in loving communion.

Praying Is Living and Living Is Praying

I now understand that I am never the one initiating prayer, much less working on it. The boundaries between living and praying are now dissolved. Praying is living, and living is praying. Since Love is the deepest, most pervasive, and central point of the universe, my initiatives originate in and are one with its initiatives. It is the initiator of my prayer and very existence. I am a participant in its movement.

Prayer is no longer God moving within me; I am now moving within God and God's amazing Dance. Prayer is no longer a way of connecting with God, because God is always connected with me and everything that surrounds me. Prayer is no longer something I do: preparation for prayer is impossible when living is praying. Prayer is not even availability on my part to which Love may respond. All of my former approaches to prayer presumed the existence of an "I-Thou" connection. Now there is no "I" trying to connect with a "Thou"; prayer is a simple awareness of Love, God, and the Dance of the universe, all rolled into one. The collapse of this "I-Thou" relationship has elicited a major reversal in my prayer. Now prayer is being held more than holding; being moved more than moving; being loved more than loving; being danced more than dancing. I experience the limitation of language as I write this last sentence, because its passive voice implies an "I" and a "Thou." So it seems best to end my limited attempt at describing prayer and communion by saying, "Love is all there is."

Our Contemplative Brain

Over time contemplation changes the brain, and in the process it heightens our awareness of Love's ways. Mike realized that God desired him to be happy with Carol. Love embraced me and desired intimacy with me, even though I was rebelling against novitiate structures and traditions. Gradually this Love changed my rebellion.

Scientific experiments in Madison, Wisconsin, highlight the same. Because the connection between science and meditation fascinates the Dalai Lama, in 1992 he invited Richard Davidson, a neurologist from the University of Wisconsin, to Dharamsala, India, for conversation. Eventually the Dalai Lama sent eight monks to Davidson's laboratory in Madison, Wisconsin. There Davidson and his colleagues used brain scanners to compare the monks' brains with those of ten students who had received one week of meditation training. The scientific data from these scans indicated that our brain is *plastic* and can be molded and changed. The scans revealed that while meditating the monks were far more alert, compassionate, and happy than the students. Comparing their scans to those of the students, it was clear that long-term meditation had permanently altered the monks' minds in measurable ways.[4]

It took a year for Mike to distinguish Jesus' Love from his mother's desire that he be a priest. Gradually, my ability to contemplate God moved me from an irritation with structures to a willingness to do anything for Love. Perhaps these stories elicit a deeper appreciation for the changes that have occurred in your prayer. Whether your contemplative practice is short or long, if you follow your deep desire for it, you will become more aware of, intimate with, and like Love and its ways.

Notes

1 Ignatius of Loyola, *The Spiritual Exercises of Saint Ignatius*, translation and commentary by George Ganss, SJ (Chicago: Loyola University Press, 1992), no. 333.

2 Julian of Norwich, *Julian of Norwich Showings*, trans. Edmund Colledge and James Walsh, Classics in Western Spirituality (New York: Paulist Press, 1978), 184.

3 Ibid., 188–89.

4 Barbara Bradley Hagerty, *Fingerprints of God* (New York: Riverhead Books, 2009), 182–85.

6

Earth Dancing

Dancing is risky, because it involves much letting go. Refined dancers know when to lead, when to be led, and when to surrender mutually to music. Power plays between partners stifle the joy of flowing freely with the music, so the most elegant dancers often sidestep control.

Praying is even riskier because the lead partner generates wildly free melodies. Human beings have only begun to explore the riches and risks of flowing with Love's grand Dance. When it comes to relying on contemplation, our deepest strength and greatest sustenance, we are all novices. We are not yet free enough to lose ourselves in untamed Love, and the boundless communion that it creates. But God understands our fear, embraces us firmly, guides us tenderly, and dances with us exuberantly.

In Chapter 3, I wrote about mystics who helped me understand aspects of this Cosmic Dance; in this chapter I write about Tom and Mary who experience this wildly free Dance in their lives. Contemplation intensifies their Love for everything and everyone.

Another Tom

Thomas Merton loved the trees and creatures that surrounded his monastery. He claimed, "It is essential to experience all the times and moods of one good place. No one will ever be able to say how essential, how truly part of a genuine life this is: but all this is lost in the abstract, formal routine or exercises under an official fluorescent light."[1] His immersion in nature strengthened his contemplation and Love of earth. It can do the same for us.

In my early visits to Monhegan I met another Tom who also values "one good place." Tom Martin's Love of earth began when he was a child. During summers his parents let him camp out at Harvey's Lake in Wilkes Barre, Pennsylvania. He would come home on the weekend, but his real home was his tent and the forest that surrounded it. His grandmother taught him how to forage for greens, seeds, nuts, and mushrooms. The solitary camping of his childhood initiated an untamed passion for earth that now influences many. During Tom's time on Monhegan, birders, photographers, and plant lovers from around the world bring specimens and their desire to understand them to Tom. Like Merton's, his contemplation reveals an extraordinary Love that moves amid all that is ordinary.

Various periodicals and newspapers have published articles about Tom Martin's photographs of birds and plants. An article titled "Really Seeing"[2] contained some of his plant photographs. A cross section of a yellow tulip nestled in a black background formed long yellow and rust-colored curves that curled tightly at their corners. Their exquisite spirals and curves would attract any artist. My favorite picture in the magazine article is a one-flowered pyrola. In this photograph a white, long-stemmed flower rises from the slide's darkness. At the end of its long white stem a tiny flower falls downward. The emergence of this delicate blossom from darkness only accentuates its simple beauty.

One photograph of a morning glory exposes Tom's depth perception. An extraordinary light emanates from its white center. As he showed it to me, he said with a wink and a smile, "This makes us believe." He had used a truck's side-view mirror to send reflected sunlight through the flower toward his camera. That amazing light leaped forth from the film and enthralled me. This man can reveal the inner life of any part of earth.

Tom and his wife, Josephine, worship in Monhegan's small chapel on Sunday mornings, but I believe nature's "good places" are his cathedral. Recently when we were chatting, he said, "Guess what amazing thing the Lord did yesterday?" He had previously told me he did not believe in God or an afterlife. I responded with, "I thought you don't believe in God." He nonchalantly said, "Oh, I go back and forth on that one."

But I have never heard Tom go back and forth while scrounging among island plants, gazing at birds through binoculars, or contemplating something with his macro lens. This self-made, very creative man who seldom uses religious language is one of the most contemplative people I know. He personifies long and loving looks at all aspects of earth. With great excitement, he once talked about having looked at a particular plant often, but he had only recently seen one of its more intricate parts. Then he said, "The best stuff is still out there; I just have to find it."

Tom never uses the language of religious experience. He would probably even shudder at the words "religious experience." But I hear Love's movement whenever he talks about earth or his photography. He once told me what happens when he photographs any piece of earth. "I truly get lost when I'm behind a camera. Its like an 'out of body' experience. This sounds corny, but I'm in another world when I'm photographing. I sound like a Buddhist, but this is the real me. I get so absorbed when I look through my lens and start to explore the inner space of something. Time stands still."

Tom tells photographers you have to love the subject matter you are photographing because then you hear its song. "If you don't like it, you won't hear the music it's singing, and no one else will either. Everything has its own song, but you have to feel it inside you. When I'm done photographing, I'm emotionally drained. There's just the camera, the object, and me. While listening to its music, I'm exhilarated. The most mundane things have a story to tell. But we're not smart enough to hear the story." What spirituality! While photographing a flower's cross section or a bird's feather, he hears their song and bows before them.

One day he talked about the way he slices his flowers and plants to photograph them. His ability to reveal the depth of tiny things never ceases to amaze me. "This is like a meditation. I really don't know what meditation is, but when I take a razor blade and cut a flower to photograph its insides, I know just how to do it. I know how much pressure is needed. Experience has made me a skilled surgeon. Each plant is genetically unique. It's up to me to slice it just right; then I can reveal its beauty. When I hit it just right, it sings to me. If I cut it wrong, it sings off-key. When it's right, it opens to me, and I get a three-part harmony. This inner exploration of my yard keeps me young. There's always something to look at out there. Me and my ten-power glass, we live in a world of fun."

Earth's Spirituality—Scientific or Empirical Evidence

Tom's contemplation nurtures his passionate Love for trees, birds, and the tiniest intricacies of flowers. Though Tom never says that all things are holy, I hear God whenever he speaks about earth's creatures. When I consider the differences between his language and mine, I am reminded that finding ways to talk about the sacred dimension of everything is a present-day challenge. But while listening to Tom and others, I realize that experience rather than analysis illuminates more about earth spirituality. Once again it is the contemplative rather than the analytical part of the brain that heightens our awareness of earth's inner life and our place within earth's communion.

I have shared my conviction that the contemplative part of Tom Martin's brain is highly developed. He often says, "I can teach people about plants, birds, and cameras, but I can't teach them how to see." Tom has a less technical way of talking about contemplation than I. He says that, if you want to see the inner beauty of something, "you have to have romance in your soul; you have to feel its rhythm. When you dance to earth's music, then you catch its inner life. I should have been a Buddhist; everything is beautiful when you are truly present to it."

Romance, rhythm, Dance, music, soul, Buddhism, and presence—this is the language of our contemplative brain. It is this part of the brain that spots a baby lamb in a pasture and has to stop the car for a longer look. The inmost self transforms a glimpse into a reverie. Our soul and its mental partners enable us to let go of personal preoccupations and celebrate any part of nature. There is a whole universe in Tom's small yard. His dancing soul and ten-power glass enable him to see a "world of fun." Through human experience we encounter a God who moves as powerfully in rocks, plants, and animals as in human beings. Through contemplative encounters we experience the sacred dimension of everything, and this insight compels us to curtsy before morning glories and one-flowered pyrolas.

Tom Martin once told me he had photographed red-headed woodpeckers for three years before taking a picture that satisfied him. To reveal the inner beauty of that bird, the feathers had to be just right, the feet properly curled, the light—that essential element of any good photograph—had to be reflected in the bird's eye. "Sometimes everything would be right, and the bird would blink. The light in its eye reveals the bird's soul, so if the bird blinks, it ruins the photograph. Then one day everything fell into place. Chimes rang, and the bird sang to me. That day a woodpecker revealed his song to me." The perfection of that photograph mattered little; the bird's inner beauty mattered greatly.

Although concepts and language limit us when we speak about a woodpecker's depth, our experience does not. Tom Martin has centered his entire life on a thrill he experiences when immersed in nature. He uses words like music, Dance, and Buddhism to explain this thrill, and I use the word spirituality. When many of us are immersed in nature, we experience the ordinary as extraordinary. These uncontrollable encounters often leave us speechless. Only gradually are we finding some language to describe the movement of Love through nature and what contemplation can add to the development of this language. When nature draws us to pray, we experience humility more than pride and surrender more than control. As Tom Martin photographed red-headed woodpeckers for three years, these birds drew him into their untamed Dancing.

Contemplating Monhegan

While acknowledging my awkward language, I focus on our *experience* of earth spirituality. Personal prayer and spiritual direction prove to me again and again that all aspects of earth are spiritual. Whether a person experiences inner healing by an ocean or deep peace during a sunrise, I hear about our uncommon encounters with nature all the time in spiritual direction. Monhegan Island is another laboratory where I explore earth's spirituality. Crucial decisions of islanders have preserved the wild beauty of this place. In safeguarding its wildness, they have sustained its spirit. I believe earth's spirit is revealed most freely in its wildness. Tom Martin is only one of the artists who have explored this island's depth; its untamed spirit has held great artists like Rockwell Kent, Edward Hopper, and James Fitzgerald in its sway since the mid-1800s.

Monhegan's wildness reveals earth's spirituality to many other people. This place mesmerizes small children with its tiny shells and gnarled seaweed and silences entire families as they sit watching a sunset from Horn Hill. People vie for a window table at the Island Inn's restaurant. A front row seat at the harbor's drama is not to be missed. The water, wind, and light lure many to some of the finest theater one could experience. Earth draws Monheganites into its sway.

One of the best proofs for the existence of human spirituality is earth itself. Spending even a short time immersed in earth can change our spirit and our demeanor. Nature's power hooks and holds our right brains and their contemplative powers. Earth helps us pray; when we let its depth affect us, it can also transform us. As contemplation helps us bow before red-headed woodpeckers, it might also transform our self-focused behaviors to earth-centered ones so we can partner Love's untamed Dance.

Contemplating Waves and Life

As a child I often watched my father bodysurf at the beach. For my father, riding a wave was an art form; he had practiced these rides so long that his body often became one with the waves. He would wait patiently for the wave that could carry him to that line where water meets sand. When he spotted the right one approaching, he maneuvered his body into its direction and waited again. As it approached, his attention was fixed on the point of greatest power, and his body was ready to leap. Once he leaped into the center of the wave, his work was done: the next few minutes were an effortless joy ride as the force of the wave carried him to the shoreline. His practice, focus, and surrender had earned him the right to these fun-loving, free, uplifting rides.

When I work with beginning spiritual directors, I liken following Love's movement to catching a wave. The controlling, letting go, and receiving of bodysurfing teaches me much about the dynamics of contemplation. When supervising or teaching, I always encourage student directors to attend to a directee's life experience and to watch, listen, and wait as patiently as my father did. I also invite them to stay on high alert, discerning which aspect of life is most filled with Love's presence. When they have aligned their attention and whole being with Love's melody, then the deeper drama begins. The quality of their presence is as crucial as their discernment of how and when to move with Love's flow. My father was one with the wave long before he leaped into it. Likewise, a spiritual director's union with Love moving in the directee enables the spiritual director to let Love carry both of them during the direction session.

Like union with a wave, it is oneness with God's presence in the other that enables a spiritual director to trust her own depth, let go of techniques, and let God's movement carry her. I am blessed with the opportunity to contemplate Love's movement in varied people during the hour in which I offer each of them spiritual direction. While listening to the pain or joy of a person's life, I often hear God drawing the directee in a certain direction. When we discern what we are hearing together, we are often pulled in a similar direction; when we focus our attention, our entire mental apparatus conspires as we catch God's wave. Depending on the strength of the person's contemplative ability and the quality of my presence, this movement can last anywhere from several to thirty minutes. The longer it lasts, the more Love pulls us into a gradual and deepening spiral. I can almost see the refined dance of millions of neurons spiraling slowly and deeply.

Watch Love with me and let it draw you into the finesse of its movement. I once offered spiritual direction to a married woman and teacher named Mary. Mary often prayed by the ocean before she came to see me, and in this session ocean waves helped her contemplate her pain. As she talks about her life since her last direction session, I am drawn to a situation that occurred with her new principal; his criticism is frightening her. She has been teaching successfully at a nearby elementary school for ten years, but there is tension between the new principal and her. Our conversation begins to focus on this tension, and as we talk, we are drawn to a deeper fear.

As we focus on her fear, she suddenly realizes the principal's criticism is reminding her of her alcoholic father. Her father began going to AA meetings when she was eight years old and remained in recovery until his death. But his erratic behavior before then had taken a toll. When he was sober he would be tender and loving, but when he drank he became critical and verbally nasty toward her mother and her. She had dealt with much of this in therapy before coming to me for spiritual direction. As we focus now on her fear, words decrease and a focused simplicity slows our pace. Though this place frightens Mary, it is easier for her to stay there because I am present with her in her fear.

As I ask her to contemplate this inner terrain, her eyes close. Mary begins to gaze more carefully at her fear, and she shares what she sees. While I encourage and evoke, she contemplates. For a while we focus on her fear and become more familiar with it. As she looks longer at her fear of her father and understands it more deeply, I begin to discern Love attracting and rerouting us. She is so focused on her fear that she cannot notice Love's presence within it, but I do. Once I sense she has greater familiarity with this interior space, I ask if she can show this part of herself and its newer content to God. She has done this with other experiences and is not surprised.

She quietly says "yes," becomes even more still, and I soon

notice tears. I ask if she wants to tell me what is happening. With eyes still closed and attention riveted, she remembers sitting at the ocean the previous day. "The ocean's gentle waves kept washing over my hurting heart; Love seemed as vast as the ocean." Keeping my words as simple as possible, so as to engage the contemplative rather than the verbal and analytical part of our brains, I say, "Let the ocean—let Love keep washing over your heart." When she says, "Love is surrounding my heart," I say, "Let it surround you." Our conversation slows down. Love is now determining the pace of our Dance. I add, "Tell me about it as it surrounds this part of you." With sparse and gradual statements she says, "It holds me. . . . I need this security. . . . I feel safe here." Our focus has shifted smoothly; it is now riveted on Love, the heart of the universe. I say, "Let it hold you. . . . Feel the safety." Again, the pace slows and words diminish. She cries softly and after a long pause says, "I need this Love . . . this holding. . . . It is so gentle . . . and strong. It washes away my fear. I need it more than I realized."

The gentle waves lead the way, and now we have become one with God's simple motion. Our letting go and letting Love lead has been gradual, but now it is complete. Love's revelation has Mary's attention, and any words from me would jar her. We instinctively become silent, as Love's music completes this Dance. I silently observe this movement happening in her by watching her face and body. My deeper self is assured that this music continues.

Ten minutes before the session ends, I gently ask her to refocus her attention on our presence with each other. She gradually lets go of her silent meditation, refocuses her mental energy, and shares what has occurred between Love and her. She shares some simple exchanges and a few realizations. Our conversation revolves around what Love has done. At one point she says, "I now have the strength to return to that situation. I can separate my principal's criticism from my father's a little better. I'll become frightened again, but next time I'll return to the ocean, and it will help me connect with Love a little more easily." Soon after this sharing, we end our direction session.

Contemplation: An Innately Human Process

This is contemplation. It is a long and loving look at the pain, fear, and joy of life. As we look, we encounter their deeper dimension, the Love that holds everything and everyone. The pace, sound, and movement of contemplation are radically different from much of the communication that occurs in daily activity. Still, any parent gazing at a child, or artist painting a landscape, or practitioner meditating at a Zen sitting, or spouse tenderly holding a partner, or lover of nature reveling in an insect experiences this innately human process. In this case Love's movement throughout the ocean catches and holds Mary's attention. Using varied means, Love draws and moves anyone who is open. As Mary contemplated Love moving throughout the ocean, its waves soothed her hurting heart. Once we let God embrace us, our consciousness simplifies and expands as we see all things as a communion.

Sometimes when I stop to pray at the ocean on blustery days, I see others sitting alone in their cars, presumably doing something similar. Have you ever sat by an ocean and felt its waves soothe your inner pain? Contemplating any part of nature, or anything for that matter, can soothe our hurts and rearrange our perspective. Because Love dances everything and everyone, our prayer and life experiences are more connected than we sometimes imagine. Sometimes being reassured that we are important and an integral part of a unified whole is enough to calm our fears and soothe our pain. Whether you enjoy music or sitting by the ocean, will you let the Love that choreographs creation wash over your heart and assure you that you are held tenderly and unconditionally in its embrace? Will you let it intensify your Love for all of creation?

Notes

1 Thomas Merton, *Conjectures of a Guilty Bystander* (New York: Doubleday, 1966), 179.

2 Susan Hand Shetterly, "Really Seeing," *Island Journal* 21 (2005): 39–43.

7

God Desiring

While searching for fulfillment of our desires, we can walk down terribly destructive paths. We fail to realize that God is the unconditional and deeply fulfilling Love we seek. Because loving and desiring are entwined, desire is one of the most powerful forces in the universe. It has also been a potent drive in the lives of my directees and in my own life. Our desire for Love is powerful, because a great-hearted Love also desires us; our desire for God is God desiring us. Contemplating our desires focuses them and leads us to their source, a desirous God.

Desiring and Being Desired

In 1965, during my first year in religious life, I began reading a book that helped me see that desiring and being desired can also be prayer. How I chose Christopher Mooney's *Teilhard de Chardin and the Mystery of Christ* from the many books on a typical convent shelf still mystifies me, but reading Mooney's writing induced me to read Teilhard's own books, *The Divine Milieu* and *The Phenomenon of Man*. It took me three years to finish these books. I was grateful for Mooney's clear and simple interpretations because Teilhard's depth far surpassed mine.

As I read these books quietly and slowly whenever I had a little time to myself, Teilhard's writing enlivened my desire for God. Much of what I say in this book has its origin in my contemplative reading of Teilhard. While writing this chapter, I realized that he had been my first spiritual director. Because

I connected with his spirituality more than what I was being taught, Teilhard's passion for God supported me in very personal ways. A line from *The Divine Milieu* had a special impact on me: "During every moment I have lived, the world has gradually been taking on light and fire for me, until it has come to envelop me in one mass of luminosity, glowing from within."[1] I had felt a "glowing" that enveloped me and drew me to religious life, though in my case it was intermingled with combativeness, as I strongly resisted this inner attraction.

For the year and a half before entering religious life, I experienced the meaning of Francis Thompson's poem, "The Hound of Heaven." Was I hounded! I had no idea whether I was desiring or being desired, but God would take hold of my heart and pull me toward religious life. Whenever the hounding quieted a little, I assumed it was over, but then it would return with a vengeance. I now know that God's desirous Love gripped my heart, pulled me into religious life, and has kept me faithful since then. Though my understanding of this universal movement was vague at best, it was my first glimpse of Love's passionate allurement. The strength and pervasiveness of that experience led me to see desire as paramount to spiritual growth and to the movement of the universe.

Until I found my first spiritual director in my mid-twenties, Teilhard's relationship with God enabled me to trust Love's early movement in me. In those first years in religious life, I had no understanding of how God was using Teilhard's desire to focus and foster mine. Now I see Love's desire for me as a caressing and fashioning of one tiny part of this grand universe, my unique heart. My early growth in desiring God and being desired by God became a conscious adventure with the help of Teilhard de Chardin's genius.

Teilhard's love of spirituality also sparked my exploration of the Christian mystical tradition. He inspired my lifelong fascination with and study of the spiritual dimension of the universe. Before reading him I had no conception of mysticism; afterwards I was fascinated by this human passion. Mysticism is no longer something I study; it has become my life. The mystics with whom I dialogue are companions, not historical figures. By including them and their desires in my writing, I honor them and their passion for God.

How is it that some people come to be called mystics? Many religious communities glean from their wisest spiritual writers those writings that will most help others connect with Love. The authors of these writings become known as mystics in the Christian tradition and by varied terms in other traditions. Teilhard de Chardin is just one of these astonishing individuals that Love has evolved to benefit our spiritual growth. I eagerly await a time when he and I meet face to face, so I can throw my arms (or whatever!) around him and share my deepest appreciation.

We Desire God

My early and forceful experience of desiring and being desired influenced my urge to offer others spiritual direction. The more I listened to others, the more I realized how central desire is to human and spiritual growth. Spiritual growth can begin with a vague awareness that something is missing in our lives, and this desire for "more" can cause us to seek a spiritual director.

Let us consider an experience of Diane, one of my directees. She had come to direction a few times when the following conversation occurred. At the time she was in her mid-thirties and a caring and competent supervisor of other nurses in a large hospital. Though successful in whatever she did, Diane said that something was missing in her life. She longed for the closeness with God that she had experienced as a child.

When I asked if she remembered instances of that childhood closeness, she told me about her mother singing lullabies and religious songs to her while she was young. She recalled liking one song that talked about God holding everything, birds that fly and her, too. I heard a great deal of emotion as she talked about God in that song and felt God drawing me to her earlier experiences. So I asked if she could remember anything about her experience of that song. I was surprised by the strength and spontaneity of her response, because during previous conversations she had emphasized God's distance.

> DIANE: I felt safe and secure as my mother sang about God holding the birds and me, but my surety about God then has left me as an adult. God seemed so caring then. I cannot believe I'm remembering this. You know what I felt the other day?
>
> JANICE: What did you feel the other day?
>
> DIANE: I didn't think of this until now. Two days ago I felt a strong desire for God welling up from somewhere deep.
>
> JANICE: That desire that came from somewhere deep, can you tell me anything more about it?
>
> DIANE: It was strong, and I felt like it was pulling me somewhere, but I didn't know where.
>
> JANICE: I'm trusting the pull. As you pay attention to it, do you notice anything else?
>
> DIANE: This is funny—it was similar to what I felt when my mother would hold me and sing to me. I don't understand this attraction—where it is coming from or going—but I feel it right now.
>
> JANICE: That attraction—just be with it for a bit.
>
> DIANE: I can't believe it. . . . I'm being loved. . . . Love is filling me and surrounding me. (Diane's words move more slowly; gradually she becomes very quiet.)

Diane and I talked more during this session, but this part of the conversation pertains to desire's dynamics. Diane's trust that something was missing in her life and her desire to experience the God of her childhood led to an experience of Love filling her. Diane is only beginning to understand how her desire can focus her on and connect her with God. Desire and Love are intertwined, and trusting one often leads to the other. In fact, our desire for Love gradually reveals a God who desires us.

God Desires Us

Have you ever desired to be near someone you love so much that you actually felt yourself being pulled toward that person? Did you ever consider that the power of that allurement might originate in a desirous God who was drawing you toward your beloved and into Love itself? I had been working with Joe, a fifty-year-old bank executive, for several years when he experienced his desire for closeness with his son as God desiring both father and son.

While watching his infant son sleep soundly one night, he began praying. His Love for Steven grew so strong that he pleaded with God to stay close to his son and keep him safe. He couldn't handle it if anything bad happened to Stevie. As we focused on this prayer, he said: "Then God's presence began filling the whole room."

JANICE: Tell me about that presence.

JOE: Love filled the room; it was holding, even rocking, Stevie and me.

JANICE: God seemed to hold and rock both of you.

JOE: Yeah! God's desire for the two of us could have knocked me over. It was so much stronger than mine for Stevie. I just knew he would never stop holding and rocking both of us.

JANICE: Pay attention to God's desire—the desire

that keeps rocking both of you.

JOE: (As Joe contemplates God's desire for Steven and him, he closes his eyes and becomes extremely quiet. Finally, he speaks slowly but definitely.) The desire I feel for Steven is so puny compared to God's desire for both of us. He can't stop rocking us, because he wants us close to himself. My desire to be close to Stevie is also God desiring both of us.

Joe had been connecting with God longer than Diane, so he already knew that his desire for God and Steven could pull him into God's Love. Whether we are loving another person or God, Love is one and the same. But Joe now knows that the source of his desire for Stevie is also God's desire for both of them. Our attraction to Love gradually reveals a God who desires us far more than we desire Him. In fact, desire and Love are cyclic dynamics. During a lifetime we gradually realize what mystics know instinctively. Desire and Love emanate from God and attract everything. We experience this deep allurement as our desire to be united with Love. Whenever we follow our deepest Loves, they pull us into God or Love itself. Our deepest desires and Loves are also God desiring and drawing us back to herself.

Infinite Desire

In my late twenties I learned a great deal about my own longing for Love and God's infinite desire for me. Then I was involved in parish ministry, and as I watched and listened to the joys and sorrows of married people, I was intensely drawn to the emotional and sexual intimacy of married life. Though the boyfriend I had dated steadily during the last two years of high school was now married and we had lost touch, I could not get him out of my mind. I suppose it was easier to become preoccupied with someone I had known rather than to conjure up someone new.

My desire to be married created a dilemma when I prayed. My relationship with God mattered, and I knew God had called me to religious life. But my longing for emotional and physical intimacy was an intensifying desire, and it preoccupied personal thoughts and prayer. So I started pleading with God to release me from my vows. As I write nearly forty years later I no longer remember the details of that daily prayer or those monthly direction sessions. Mostly I would sit in our convent chapel, imagine intimacy with a man, and beg God to call me to married life.

But I vividly remember the prayer that resolved this terrible tension. After wrestling with these longings for over a year, I went on my annual eight-day retreat and struggled with the same urges throughout the retreat. Yet by the end my director and I knew nothing had been resolved. God wanted me to stay in religious life, and I still wanted to leave, meet someone, and marry him.

Then God changed my need to leave religious life. While praying outside on the last night of retreat, my prayer seemed as dim as the colonnade under which I paced. I had been telling God that my emotional and sexual needs would not go away, so I could not imagine how I would find happiness while remaining celibate. Suddenly in the midst of my talking, God simply said, "I'll keep you faithful."

My first response was surprise and annoyance. I said in reply, "That's not what I'm asking for!" But then I noticed something more important: it was the way God said, "I'll keep you faithful," that changed me that night. Love's fathomless longing filled my heart and body; it pulled me into an intimacy I could not have imagined before this experience. This intimate Love was simple, ardent, and deep. I knew God wanted me, wanted me to be celibate, and wanted all of this passionately. His longing for closeness changed me. All of my resistance melted before God's infinite desire. In my late twenties I had assumed I needed another human being to fill my deepest needs and had doubted God's ability to do so. That night God's infinite passion convinced me that Love was boundless and would fill my yearning for profound Love.

After that conversion, whenever I experienced a deep desire for Love, I would expose my longing to God and wait watchfully for his response. I would sometimes experience his fervent emotion moving deeply within me, but mostly I felt a simple and deep Love filling my neediness. I appreciated what time I could find for solitude, because then we could quietly and mutually share Love in my depth.

While listening to so many different people in spiritual direction, I have learned that our desirous God embraces all of us and wants us to know how tightly we are held. Paying attention to others' desires and to my own has taught me that contemplation is more than peaceful gazing and loving encounters; it is also desiring and being desired. Diane's, Joe's, and my stories show how contemplation focuses our desires on Love. This centering reveals God's fathomless desire for everything and everyone. Gradually our passion for everything and everyone intensifies and becomes a little more like God's. Contemplation pulls us into Love's ardent allurement of the universe.

A God of Eros

That God desires us passionately is one of the best kept secrets of the Christian tradition. But Bernard McGinn, the author of a series on Christian mysticism, exposes this powerful aspect of Christian spirituality. Origen, who was born around 185 C.E., was the first Christian mystic to develop a theology of God as Eros. McGinn explains how God's gradual transformation of human desiring (eros ii) into God's desiring (Eros I) becomes a key theme in Origen's theology.[2] Then as McGinn develops his series on the history of *The Presence of God,* we realize that many Christian mystics experienced and wrote about a desirous God. God's passion is a prevalent part of the Christian spiritual tradition.

I most appreciate the feminine dimension that Julian of Norwich, a fourteenth-century English mystic, brings to the cycling of divine and human desire. Julian writes about a desirous God who is both our Father and our Mother and human beings who are filled with fathomless longing. Some contemporary psychotherapists say we are longing for our mother's Love or yearning to return to her womb. Although Julian never minimizes the role of mothers, she claims that it is God, our Mother, for whom we really long. A mother's Love can be an icon that reminds us of the primordial passion that bonds the entire universe. Human beings desire union with each other, earth itself, and the depth that dances everything. Julian writes repeatedly about our "compelling desire to be wholly united into him . . . that will last until the day that we die, still longing for love."[3]

She also uses God's words to remind us that God is the source and the fulfillment of our yearning. "I am he, the great supreme goodness of every kind of thing; I am he who makes you to love; I am he who makes you to long; I am he, the endless fulfilling of all true desires."[4] She also reveals Love's thirst for us and the role it plays in our lives. "So truly is there in God a quality of thirst and longing; and this is the characteristic of spiritual thirst, which will persist in him so long as we are in need, and will draw us up into his bliss."[5]

A Desirous Cosmos

The drama of desire is larger than the human species. When I woke from anesthesia, I immediately sensed its power pulsing through the earth and the entire universe. Though I was in a single-bed hospital room for two weeks, unable to do much of anything but visit with my parents once a day, I was never lonely. My body was extremely disabled, but my spirit danced intimately with my family, friends, and Sisters of Mercy around the world. The reverse is also true. An alluring universe was also dancing me. A desirous Love filled that small hospital room, connecting me with everything and everyone. From that point onward Love compelled me to speak and write about the relatedness of human, earth, and cosmic desire.

When Brian Swimme speaks about allurement and the magnetism of the universe in his DVD set, *The Powers of the Universe*, I begin to Dance. Swimme admits that gravity mystifies him. He has focused much of his study on this powerful pull that draws and holds everything. For him gravity and its allurement are two of the universe's most powerful attractions.

Then he gets specific. I sit in rapt attention as he talks about the gravitational bond between the sun, earth, and one tiny molecule. Over three billion years ago, the sun and earth began bonding with each other. As he talks about this bonding, I feel as though I have a front-row seat at the grandest story ever told. I easily imagine the graceful movement of hydrogen, carbon dioxide, the sun's radiant light, and earth, as they are drawn to and bond with each other. In this theater of the unexpected, a miracle happens. The chlorophyll molecule is born, and earth and sun develop a new intimacy with each other.

There was no chlorophyll molecule when earth began. We are only beginning to grasp the details of its advanced interactions. Swimme becomes quite animated when he says, "This is a *really* advanced form of creativity." He emphasizes that individual beings without brains invented this intricate creation. So much for brains! But they did have the capacity for invention and the capability to deepen the intimacy between the earth and its sun. Now plants draw in sunlight for their nourishment and the entire planet's.

So there I am in a front-row seat in the theater of the unexpected. Evolution's ballet has achieved one more stupendous miracle, and I am awed. A tiny molecule that has baffled the best minds for centuries is invented. On this evolutionary stage a tiny molecule intensifies the attraction of earth and sun. The stupendous sun, its grand planet earth, and this tiny creation dance with utmost finesse. They glide to the music of allurement, and faithfully embrace their intimacy. This is the finest theater that I know.

We human beings easily forget that gravity holds us, and the sun continuously attracts us. Perhaps we never acknowledge the alluring intimacy within which we are immersed or that these dynamics have some similarity to human desiring. In my way of seeing, Love desires, draws, and holds all things, even tiny but mighty molecules. Sometimes our human needs and perspectives cause us to forget that Love also dances chlorophyll. If it ceased to function, our species and many others would die.

Joy fills me in this theater, as I watch the sun, earth, plants, and photosynthesis take their bow. I applaud them and Brian Swimme, their superb narrator. In return I bow before them, and the Love that allures and dances them. How could we ever see God's Love as a polite, placid sort of emotion? The mystics had it right: only a wildly free and lusty Eros could allure and hold a sun, earth, and chlorophyll molecule. Though I listened to Brian Swimme's version of the Cosmic Dance nearly two decades after my brain surgery, it was one more celebration of what Love showed me when I awoke from anesthesia. During my long-term recovery from brain surgery, contemplating God's allurement of the sun, its planet earth, and the tiniest creatures gave abundant meaning to each and every day, and Brian Swimme has given me one more way to integrate human, earth, and cosmic spirituality.[6]

Eros and a Carolina Wren

The day before Easter in 1958, Thomas Merton was wrestling in his journal with the way words, propositions, and analyses sometimes hide God from us. Then he remembered a Carolina wren that had landed on his shoulder the previous day, while he was outside reading. The wren had then hopped on the corner of his book and paused to look at him before it flew away.

Imagine the sheer joy of sitting in the woods and having a wren land on the book you are reading. Merton's journal reflection on this charming Carolina wren demonstrates how Eros lures and holds our contemplative mind. With great seriousness he was grappling with that part of our brain that knows *about* creation. Then in flew a wren! That wild and wonderfully free bird drew him into the Cosmic Dance; instantly Merton experienced union.

Who of us would not be amazed if a bird landed on the corner of our book, looked into our eyes, then flew away? Merton instantly moved from his analytical to his dancing brain. Nature has a way of doing this to us.

I have been attracted to Carolina wrens since I read of Merton's familiarity with one. Weather permitting, I sometimes write on the porch of the apartment I rent on Monhegan Island. Since the porch is elevated and immersed in the island's shrubs and trees, many creatures afford me brief and delightful breaks from writing. One morning I was quite lucky to spot a Carolina wren investigating all the nooks and crannies on my porch. It eventually perched on the rail only ten feet away. Listening to it repeatedly sing variations of the same theme, I understood those who find this song among the finest of bird species and was entranced.

When the singing began, the wren's body nearly doubled in size as music engulfed and expanded it. Its breast swelled as each feather stood out and filled the surrounding space. I had no doubt that this creature was singing to a nearby spouse. It held me spellbound as it quivered from joy. I was pulled into its full-bodied, erotic abandonment; such magnanimous giving collapses divisions between species. That Carolina wren and I, along with heaven and earth, were one.

Magnanimity, whatever its source, evokes contemplation; it forces us to slow down and take a long and loving look. If we humans take care while beholding another, we often encounter the deeper dimension of the universe, and gazing upon this transforms us into the passionate Love we contemplate. Eros allures, bonds, and dances all of us with great exultation; when we contemplate anything, our desire intensifies, and we surrender to a wildly free Dance. Mystics and wrens experience the deeper aspect of the universe more clearly because they let Eros woo them.

Have you ever experienced a bird singing only ten feet away to a hidden mate? If so, did it pull you into its lively and lusty song? While you contemplate anything, Love is focusing your attractions, intensifying your desire, and enabling you to dance with birds, plants, and people. As your desire intensifies over time, our desirous God will draw you more easily into the liveliest, lustiest, freest Dance I know. This Dance has nothing to do with eroticism, and everything to do with unbounded, untamed Love. This passion strengthens our intimacy with all things and makes us more like Love itself. We have only begun to explore what can happen to our desire when we steadily contemplate a God of Eros.

Notes

1 Pierre Teilhard de Chardin, *The Divine Milieu* (New York: Harper and Row, 1960), 13.

2 Bernard McGinn, *The Foundations of Christian Mysticism* (New York: Crossroad, 1991), 125.

3 Julian of Norwich, *Julian of Norwich Showings*, trans. Edmund Colledge and James Walsh, Classics in Western Spirituality (New York: Paulist Press, 1978), 255.

4 Ibid., 296.

5 Ibid., 231.

6 Brian Swimme, *The Powers of the Universe*, DVD (San Francisco, Calif.: Center for the Story of the Universe, 2004).

8

Vulnerability Accepted

The horrors of September 11, 2001, exposed the terrible vulnerability of being human. Yet frailty can waken human beings to their spiritual depth. As I pondered the experiences of Marian Fontana, who lost her husband that day, I watched God use her vulnerability to deepen her prayer and her connection with Love. Contemplating our vulnerability can strengthen and expand our Love, and any increase of Love is also a deepening of spirituality.

Embracing Emptiness

Marian Fontana screamed and fell to the floor as she watched the South Tower collapse on television. Because Dave, her husband and a New York City firefighter, was in a specialized department, she knew that she had lost him. Marian said Dave was a sculptor, a historian, and "a beautiful spirit." He was also an "incredible father" who sacrificed many things so he could spend time with Aidan, their son. *Faith and Doubt at Ground Zero*, a DVD that asked some deeper questions about people's experience of September 11, included photographs of this hulk of a man and his small son, making this tragedy even more poignant. Those of us who saw this DVD shared in that family's uproarious fun and their quieter, more tender times.

The months that followed were especially painful for Marian. She attended fourteen wakes and funerals of other firefighters, and planned Dave's memorial service for October 17, his birthday. Finally on December 6 she traveled to Hawaii with other firefighters. It was the first time they could relax a little and enjoy something, but when she returned to her hotel room by herself, the stark reality of everything hit her. Dave's death created an agonizing vacuum within her.

> I couldn't believe that this God that I talked to in my own way for thirty-five years could make the most beautiful place in the world, and turn this loving man into bones. I couldn't reconcile the difference between those two extremes. I guess that's when I felt that my faith was so weakened by the 11th. I felt like God was just not present in me the way it had been. I guess all I feel at this point is the profound absence of Dave and my conversations with God that I used to have and don't have anymore.
>
> I used to talk quietly to God. I said "thank you for Dave—thank you for Aidan—thank you for my life. God bless everyone—God bless the children—please heal the sick"; you know the usual blessings. And now I can't bring myself to speak to him anymore because I feel so abandoned. I guess deep down inside I know He still exists, and that I have to forgive, and move on, but I'm not ready to do that yet.[1]

Marian agonizes over Dave's absence and God's abandonment. My experience of listening to others tells me it takes time for agony like this to diminish significantly, and for the hole it creates to fill gradually. Marian begins this process by sharing her abandonment with friends. Within this profound turmoil Love moves and creates, but very slowly. The deeper the loss, the longer the period of recovery. Marian Fontana lost the Love of her life and the God with whom she talked in her own way. I have found that the emptiness left by loss is God's domain. Love moves slowly, with utmost respect for the loss, but also moves steadily. It can draw a person into a deeper way of relating, and into a more profound approach to meaning.

Contemplative Glimmers

Several years after September 11 Marian Fontana wrote *A Widow's Walk*. The book is about a courageous woman, a loving man, and the fervor of their relationship. Here we can contemplate God's transformation of vulnerability into spirituality, into Love.

Marian wrote about widows and firefighters who agonized over lost loved ones and searched for renewed connections with their dead husbands and friends. One conversation between Marian and Theresa Russo, a friend and another widow, highlighted aspects of our spiritual self. Marian listened half-heartedly as Theresa said she was getting many signs of Mike's presence. Theresa sometimes began these conversations with, "I know you think I'm nuts," and this time Marian responded with, "I'd love to believe that every light flicker or song on the radio is him. . . . I want something a little more clear. I want to know where he is and what he's feeling and everything I used to . . . I just want that so bad . . . I just . . . need . . . to know he's okay up there." Suddenly she began to cry.

Theresa squeezed her hand and said, "I know. It kills me. *It kills me*. . . . Listen, I was a nurse for fifteen years and spent a lot of time around dying people. I *know* they're in a better place. . . . Dying people all do the same thing. They call out for people that have gone before them, they get really, really serene, and if you saw that day after day, you wouldn't wonder where Dave is."[2]

Marian wanted to respond, but refrains from a song were floating through the restaurant. She heard Etta James's unique voice singing her signature song, "At Last." She bit her lip to keep it from quivering, and told Theresa it was her wedding song. Her friend smiled "like a cat with a mouse." "You see? Don't tell me that's coincidence. You're just not open to seeing signs. They're all around us." As Theresa shared some of her more recent and frequent signs, Marian ate her steak, and quietly said, *"Thank you, Dave."*[3]

Marian sometimes doubted these "signs," but I have learned that faith includes doubt. I also see the search for the presence of a dead loved one as a spiritual process. My long-term experience of offering spiritual direction has convinced me that human beings do sense the presence of those who have died. Our contemplative power connects us with much more than is visible; it reveals earth's deepest dimension.

During her eulogy of Dave, Marian looked at her young son in the pew and said, "Aidan, love is the only thing that lasts forever."[4] The Love that flowed among Marian, Dave, and Aidan never ends. Love is more powerful than death; on this I stake everything. Wherever Love is, there also is God; Love and God are one and the same. Love and God communicate themselves continually, and so do those immersed in Love, whether living or dead. Those of us who still live on this side of death, need only to learn and trust the language of this aspect of Love. Marian and her friends are learning to contemplate their loved ones who have died. *A Widow's Walk* reveals aspects of Love's deepest language.

When Marian shared stories about Aidan's connections with his dead father, I recalled *A Window to Heaven,* a book I had read ten years earlier about the epiphanies of dying children. Those children had no theological knowledge, only vivid descriptions of a special presence in their lives. As they moved through their dying process, they talked spontaneously about angels singing, Jesus coming, and other experiences and dreams. An eight-year-old with cancer dreamt about a yellow school bus. Jesus was on it, told him about his impending death, and invited him to come with him on the bus. He peacefully shared this dream with his parents shortly before he died. Children's spiritual connections can often be simpler and more direct than those of adults.[5]

When Dave's memorial service was over, their limousine drove past rows of firefighters standing in a firm salute. Marian saw chins trembling and tears flowing as the firefighters watched Aidan. He was leaning out the window wearing his father's fire hat and saluting all of them in return. Aidan suddenly said to her, "I see Daddy." The church steps had cleared of people, and he was pointing at them. Marian asked where he was, and her son responded, "Right there. He's giving the thumbs-up."[6]

One night, before the service, Marian was reading *Star Wars* to her son for the umpteenth time. Between his fidgeting and a bed crowded with stuffed animals, she was physically uncomfortable. Finally when his foot landed hard on her shin, she impatiently got up to move a rocker closer so she could read comfortably. Aidan whined,

> "Don't sit there! . . . There's someone sitting there already."
>
> I feel my brow furrow. "Who?"
>
> "It's a firefighter angel."
>
> A chill trickles down my back like cold water. "Is it Daddy?" I ask.
>
> "No. He has firefighter clothes on and wings."
>
> "Oh, like the picture we have?" I say, deflating.
>
> "No, his clothes aren't dirty and he's not sad. It's one of Daddy's friends."
>
> "Who," I ask, trying not to sound desperate, but it is too late. Aidan is finished with this conversation.
>
> "Keep reading," he insists, and so I slide back into bed with him, not wanting to sit on an angel![7]

What a moving exchange between mother and son! Her words about "not wanting to sit on an angel" bespoke courtesy and awe before simple yet profound epiphany. Gems fall from the mouths of babes! If only we could trust that Love lasts forever and is much more vast than we imagine. As adults become more childlike, they too accept the presence of "firefighter angels." Deepening spirituality joins heaven and earth. It also reveals to adults the deepest language imaginable, the language of contemplation.

Contemplative Presence

Marian had written comedy, screenplays, and articles, but writing a eulogy for her husband was radically different. At first she struggled with what to say. "How am I going to sum up seventeen years with my best friend, my husband? How can simple words express how huge my love is?"[8] But soon she began listing the things that Dave loved, and sentences began forming themselves around these words. "A snowstorm of memories and thoughts and feelings is coming quicker. They are a tide rising up under my fingers. Click. Click. Click. I can feel Dave's presence in the kitchen and I inhale him in deeply, like hot steam. It is after three. I have been writing for three hours but I am finished, and it is done."[9]

What an amazing description of the duet of life and death. She inhaled Dave's presence, "like hot steam." How much simpler and more ordinary can religious experience get?

The people I listen to in spiritual direction often experience God's presence in the ordinary aspects of life. They can begin by telling me about a simple conversation, and, as they talk, they realize Love is there revealing itself in these earthy encounters. Love can use a falling leaf to encourage a father to loosen his control over his teenage son or a calm ocean to say to a harried administrator, "Come rest in me a little more often." Here is one of the greatest challenges of modern life: we are all immersed in Love, but we do not attend to its presence. I find that the heart beating at the center of the universe more often communicates in typically human ways. Dave communicated Love to his son and wife through a simple, clear awareness of his presence. His response to Marian's and Aidan's vulnerability was strengthening and expanding their Love. Their suffering was teaching them how to pray.

On the Lookout

All my teachers and supervisors taught me to be on the lookout for God's responses to honest sharing. They saw prayer as a relationship, and they were especially sensitive to Love's response in that relationship. In our human relationships we are accustomed to back and forth communication. The depth of a relationship is directly related to the mutual sharing of our thoughts, emotions, and lives. We too often forget that the same mutuality is central to prayer. When we pray, we need to share life and our reactions to it with God. We also need to watch and wait for Love's response to these reactions. Prayer works when we are open to the universe's deepest dimension and its capacity to communicate with us. The uniqueness of each reply, tailor-made to the situation being prayed with, has often surprised me.

Because my ministry calls me to stay on the lookout and wait for the appearance of the spiritual self, my deeper self leaped within me when Marian Fontana said she felt Dave's presence in her kitchen. I danced inside when she inhaled him. Dave Fontana was revealing his new life to his wife and son, and in the process he also exposed the simple, direct, and reciprocal nature of contemplation.

For the widows of firefighters, wakes and funerals blended into one massive experience of sadness and pride. Marian wrote about the wake and funeral of Mike Esposito, the lieutenant of Mike's squad. All the firefighters, especially Dave, appreciated his humor and respected his leadership. At the wake Timmy Rogers, a firefighter friend working "at the site," told Marian they had found the remains of Mike Esposito. "He was in really bad shape. We only know it was him because of the jacket and the list of guys working that was in his pocket. Other than that—it might take a while to confirm DNA, so we have to keep it quiet."[10] Inwardly Marian wondered if Dave had been working close to Mike, and if he would be recognizable. First she had hoped Dave was alive; then she hoped he would be found; finally she hoped he would not be in too many pieces. Now she imagined Mike's jacket, black and flat, "like the Wicked Witch after she had melted away."[11]

All the funerals were terribly sad. Mike Esposito's brothers sobbed through their eulogies. Marian was proud of Denise, Mike's wife, as she gave her husband's eulogy. Marian knew their Love was unique and special, like Dave's and hers. While Denise read her eulogy, Marian suddenly saw Dave's face next to Mike's and "they were laughing like two little boys." She wrote, "The image is so clear and intense it frightens me. I blink hard, am I so overwrought that I am seeing things? I close my eyes, trying hard to put the image away, but there they are again: Mike's and Dave's faces smiling beautifully, as if they are right in front of me."[12]

This is what I hear so often while listening to others in spiritual direction. The life situations that are prayed with vary, but sharp distinctions between heaven and earth, death and life, divinity and humanity, daily events and deeper realities collapse during spiritual encounters. At a terribly sad event Marian suddenly sees Mike and Dave laughing like little boys "as if they are right in front of me."

Being as honest as Marian Fontana when we pray is important because sharing our emotion with God is necessary if we want the spiritual part of us to grow strong. Equally important is our ability to perceive God's response to prayer. Dave and Mike expose the porous nature of life and death. Noticing interior movements, the language of Love, is crucial to deepening spirituality. If we want to consciously participate in the Cosmic Dance, we must be aware of its language and communication with us.

The Choice of September 11th

The women and men in this chapter are suffering horrible loss because of an evil act. Growing spiritually offers great joy, but it also requires acceptance of vulnerability. There is an integral relationship between Marian's anguish and her exquisite epiphanies. There are times in our lives when the vulnerability of deep pain or joy creates permeability within us. This heated psychic condition enables us to see more deeply. Everything becomes transparent before us, highlighting its inner and often hidden life.

The way we relate to the vulnerability of being human influences our connection with our spiritual self and the Love that resides there. We have watched how Marian's experience of agonizing loss forced her to search for a new way of connecting with Dave and God. When Dave reveals himself to her, her experience and understanding of Love expands. Contemplation refines vulnerability by strengthening and expanding our Love; vulnerability embraced is spirituality deepened.

Marian's experience says much to us about the importance of finitude and its vulnerability. In an instant the frailty of being human fell upon her. She could not hide from this reality. As she dealt with this part of being human, she resisted God but instinctively reached out to Dave—to Love. Her search can guide us. In order to live happily and peacefully, we sometimes try to protect ourselves with excessive activity, high productivity, technological prowess, or a military machine. But in a time when a terrorist can make a dirty bomb, we desperately need Love's uncommon wisdom.

I found this uncommon wisdom in the documentary *Faith and Doubt at Ground Zero*. The final section of this documentary was simple and strong. The skeletal remains of the Towers appeared first with that horrid smoke swirling around them. Then came those ethereal beams of blue light that streamed from Ground Zero, disappearing into the night sky. These two images kept fading into each other. The camera panned both scenes from all angles as the images danced to the music of Samuel Barber's *Adagio for Strings*. Then several anonymous voices mingled with the music. They reflected on the couple that had joined hands and leaped from the South Tower; our minds grope for meaning even in God-awful events.

The first speaker saw only despair in their jump, and I understood his perspective. The next two voices were filled with hope. I recognized one as the distinctive voice of Monsignor Lorenzo Albacete, a Catholic priest. As he spoke, photographs of stars, planets, gases, and vast darkness filled the screen, and blue, orange, and red light gleamed before viewers. In every incredible photograph of darkness and light, light overcame darkness.

Monsignor Albacete's words were interwoven with the splendor of celestial light. In the middle of his statement, just as he encouraged us to make a choice, the music changed. The *Adagio* that had soothed us in our grief became a quieter, subtler, more uplifting melody. Monsignor encouraged us to contemplate the couple that had joined hands and fell into the unknown.

> To me that image is an inescapable provocation—this gestureless holding of hands in the midst of that horror. It embodies what September 11th was all about. The image confronts us with a need to make a judgment—a choice. Does it show the ultimate hopelessness of human attempts to survive the power of hatred and death? Or is it an affirmation of a greatness within our humanity itself that somehow shines in the midst of that darkness, and contains the hint of a possibility—a power greater than death itself? Which of the two? It's a choice. It's the choice of September 11th.[13]

If we engage personal and communal vulnerability, it forces us to choose. Does the prevalent vulnerability of the universe and its earth community lead its human species toward despair and meaninglessness? Or does it elicit hope in a Love that is far beyond human cognition and imagination? I believe the authors of this amazing video opted for the latter choice. Monsignor Albacete certainly made a choice. He saw that leap as "the hint of a possibility—a power greater than death itself."

The words from another, less recognizable, voice preceded Monsignor Albacete's. Because I thought their contemplation exposed our deeper self with great precision, I tried hard to identify the speaker behind the voice. My best listening skills connected the sound of the voice with Reverend David Benke, a Lutheran minister. He also found hope in that couple's jump.

> I try to whisper prayers for the sudden dead, the harrowed families of the dead, and the screaming souls of the murderers. But I keep coming back to his hand in her hand, nestled in each other with such extraordinary, ordinary, naked love. It's the most powerful prayer I can imagine, the most elegant, the most graceful. It's everything we are capable of against horror and loss and tragedy. It's what makes me believe that we're not fools to believe in God. To believe that human beings have greatness and holiness within them, *like seeds that open only under great fire.* To believe that who we are persists past what we were. *To believe against evil evidence hourly that love is why we are here.*[14] (Emphasis added.)

Contemplating human and cosmic vulnerability refines it, it helps us experience and accept a stronger, more expansive, and unconditional Love. We have diverse understandings of this universal power. Regardless of our religious affiliation or the lack of it, I believe many of us can trust that Love itself is a force that is greater than that of all human beings combined. Love is why we are here. But we need to choose it, because Love is supremely courteous; it never forces itself on anyone.

Extreme and Graceful Dancing

With fire at their backs, a man and woman confront an ungodly choice. Incineration or disintegration—what a hideous choice! But I see a deeper dynamic in their decision making. They are forced to confront frailty, bypass control, hold hands, and leap into the unknown. What happens next is beyond their control.

What can I say about their agonizing Dance and its horrible finale? None of us knows their motivation, nor do we know precisely what happens after death. Still, I am aware of our spiritual self, and can it dance! My work with the deepest part of us tells me that there is no violence, fire, or death in our soul. Deep within us there is only the mutual give and take of wildly free dancers. When that couple stepped out, I believe they fell into a Cosmic Dance. This dynamic takes evil and makes goodness, takes hatred and makes Love. Untamed Love is the deepest dimension of this universe; it surpasses our wildest dreams and overcomes our most horrendous violence.

Love moves through everything, but vulnerability is one of its favored venues. Marian fell to her knees in the face of agonizing loss, and Love gradually transformed her vulnerability by deepening her prayer and expanding her Love. Have life's agonies ever forced you to your knees in prayer? If so, you have much in common with Marian and everyone else. In this chapter we watched Marian's connection with Dave change over time. I encourage you to stay on the lookout for Love's responses to your prayer. Contemplation refines vulnerability by deepening our prayer and expanding our Love. In the deep encounter contemplation elicits, vulnerability accepted becomes spirituality deepened.

Notes

1 Helen Whitney and Ron Rosenbaum, *Faith and Doubt at Ground Zero* (New York: PBS DVD Video, 2002).

2 Marian Fontana, *A Widow's Walk* (New York: Simon and Schuster, 2005), 208–9.

3 Ibid., 209.

4 Ibid., 180.

5 Diane M. Komp, M.D., *A Window to Heaven* (Grand Rapids, Mich.: Zondervan, 1992), 88.

6 Fontana, *Widow's Walk*, 182.

7 Ibid., 154–55.

8 Ibid., 159.

9 Ibid.

10 Ibid., 251.

11 Ibid., 251.

12 Ibid., 254.

13 Whitney and Rosenbaum, *Faith and Doubt*.

14 Ibid.

9

Vulnerability Refined

While interviewing theologians, sociologists, and psychiatrists, Barbara Bradley Hagerty concluded that brokenness elicited conversion more than anything else. When, through addiction, cancer, loneliness, unemployment, illness, or indefinable misery, people have exhausted their resources and experienced defeat, they often "surrender, and in that release, they find a calm. It is the only way that many stubborn souls find God."[1]

The weakness that is part of being human can force us to reach for a strength that is greater than our own. We are a finite and interdependent communion; contemplation refines our vulnerability by helping us accept our need for and reliance on each other, earth, and God. Contemplation humbles us so we can act as if we are part of untamed communion. Let's watch how Love used the limitations that accompanied my brain surgery to help me accept our reliance on Love and its vast relatedness.

God Comforts Us

I will never forget two hospital experiences. Several days after the surgery I was scheduled for a CAT scan and had waited all day for that x-ray. At 8 p.m. I was finally wheeled down to the hospital basement on a stretcher and placed near the CAT scan room. I was left there alone, at night, in an inhospitable basement, with a helpless body. I could do little more than wait, so I waited and waited and waited.

I could hear several technicians doing nothing but chatting and laughing, so I was not frightened. But after an hour of patient waiting, I became angry enough to do what I thought impossible. All the bars on the stretcher were raised. So not knowing if my one eye, extreme imbalance, impaired brain, or utter weakness would disable me, I slithered through the narrow space between the bottom bars, inched across the ten-foot-wide hallway, grabbed the bar on the wall, and struggled to the open doorway.

I leaned against the doorframe and must have looked a sight with my huge eye patch, partially shaved head, sagging body, and flimsy hospital gown. My anger was apparent as I asked the technicians why they were not x-raying me, so I could return to my room for the rest I needed. A young woman immediately came to my aid. As she helped me to the stretcher, she explained that they had been instructed to delay all x-rays (there was only mine to delay). A man had been shot in the head, was in surgery, and would soon need an x-ray. Now I understood, but it would have helped greatly if they had told me why I had to wait so long. The poor man was soon x-rayed and my scan followed his.

By the time they had lifted me from the stretcher to my own bed, I lay there motionless. Two hours of waiting alone, with a helpless body, on a lifeless corridor, for an undetermined time had drained me of the little strength I had possessed. Finding energy for anything, including prayer, proved impossible, so God did the praying for me. With utmost sensitivity, a delicate affection moved throughout my body. My body was terribly weak, and this Love soothed and comforted me. All I could do was pay attention. Even that did not last long, because I soon fell asleep. Extreme vulnerability revealed a Love on which I could rely. Whether or not we know it, Love embraces us softly, especially when we are too weak to embrace anything.

God Carries Us

A few days later I suffered through a difficult MRI of my brain. This procedure was much longer and far more difficult than the CAT scan. Because of pain in my lower back, I had received other

MRIs. I used them to pray, so they had never been a problem for me. Still, this one was radically different. Laying my freshly stitched head on a metal surface for over one hour was sheer torture: each stitch felt like a knife blade piercing the center of my brain. The only thing they could use to cushion my incision was a thin sheet. Needless to say, it was useless. After twenty minutes of quiet endurance, I asked the technician to stop the MRI. I could no longer handle the pain. His encouragement fooled me into thinking that we were close to the end. His care and conversation enabled me to endure agonizing pain long enough to finish the test.

The next day my parents came for their daily visit. Though the anguish of the previous day had disappeared, I was so drained of energy that I could not speak. My parents understood my inability to converse, and silence enveloped us. This quietude was uplifting because it was inundated with God. Silence permeated the room and was so thick it seemed we could have cut through it. At one point the Love that engulfed all of us made me smile. My father asked why I was smiling, and I told him I was enjoying their Love for me and mine for them.

Sometimes prayer becomes deep insight, and so it was with this prayer. Contemplation helps us see a little more like God sees. The Love that I saw when I wakened from anesthesia enabled me to see my parents' Love more clearly. I recalled the numerous times when my mother cared for me while I was sick and my father's early risings so he could drive us to school before he went to work. But mainly I saw their self-sacrificing Love for each other, their children, and grandchildren. Their limitations paled before their goodness. No words that I know of can describe their Dance in that deep silence. God embraced them; they embraced us; and we all moved freely in a most serene Dance.

In that silence I saw Love carrying my parents and them carrying us into and beyond adulthood. Their Love also cradled me and my terribly impaired body. Sometimes we are called to carry others, and other times we are meant to be carried; that is how an interdependent and loving communion works. As I write, my parents are in their early nineties and becoming less self-sufficient. Though they are strong for their age, we carry them a little more than we did when they were younger.

The Love that I saw in my parents' relationship is only a shadow of the Love that dances earth and the universe. Contemplating vulnerability humbles us, and then we see more clearly how God carries everything and everyone—forever.

God Is Tender toward Us

Four months after the surgery I visited my neurosurgeon for the second time. The nurse in charge asked me to visit a man who had experienced the same surgery two months after me, because she thought that seeing what two more months of healing could accomplish might encourage him. As soon as I entered the room where he waited, I saw something I had not expected. He was a handsome, well-dressed man, perhaps in his sixties. His impeccable navy blue suit and thick white hair only accentuated his good looks. I assumed the attractive younger woman to his right was his daughter. But his elegant appearance contrasted with his fallen face. The flesh of his entire left cheek was sagging beneath his lower jawbone. I knew immediately what had happened. His seventh cranial nerve, the one that governs facial muscles, had not survived the surgery. Though he was handsome and stylish, his fallen face stood out.

I immediately embraced and then addressed this saddened man, "I know something of what you have been through." The poignancy of our meeting pushed pleasantries aside. Words meant little to the two of us; our impromptu, empathic embrace said it all. I felt great empathy for this handsome man who had not been as fortunate as I. The muscles on the right side of my face were temporarily paralyzed, but my cheek had not fallen. My body's symptoms had enabled an early diagnosis. The prompt removal of the tumor prevented it from growing around and destroying the seventh cranial nerve, the one that controls facial muscles.

His left eye also caught my attention. The muscles in my right eyelids were still sluggish and heavy when I tried to blink. His eyelids looked perfect. He told me that the nerve that opened and closed his eyelids had been destroyed during the operation, and weeks later a plastic surgeon had operated on his eyelids. She wove the thin wires of a V-shaped spring inside the edge of each eyelid. The tiny circular spring at its base was implanted in the corner of his eye, and it enabled him to open and close his eyelids. He said this procedure was the only one that produced pain. The brain surgery was debilitating, but of itself it caused little pain.

The same eye surgeon had strongly advised me to have this spring implanted in my eyelids, because she was sure they would not shut on their own. I had decided to wait and work with them on my own. It was a wise decision. Now, many years later, my eyelids often feel heavy and awkward, but they still close on their own power. Thankfully I never needed that awful sounding operation, because the surgery itself could have destroyed the recovering nerve.

My connection with that handsome man was deep but brief, so I will never know if he found our meeting encouraging, as the nurse had hoped. But I will never forget him or our tender embrace. I sensed the rarest tenderness encircling both of us. God's compassion for us in our weakness spotlights a Love that is both tender and strong.

While offering others spiritual direction, I have witnessed similar softheartedness. When someone is angry with a friend, fearful of a boss, hurt by a spouse, confused as a leader, ashamed of having hurt another or of having been personally abused, God often responds with great tenderness toward acknowledged human limitation. The more deeply we accept our brokenness, the more tenderly Love responds. I have never seen God condemn us for being fallible or vulnerable, especially when we embrace our weakness.

Gratitude

When I left the doctor's office that day, I felt great empathy for that man and gratitude that my seventh nerve was healing without an implant that could have destroyed the nerve. From the moment I woke from surgery, I experienced overwhelming gratitude. Of course there were times when the slow recovery caused boredom or physical pain triggered agony, but gratitude was never far away. When I saw the neurosurgeon during my four-month visit, I thanked him for saving my life. Without his successful removal of my tumor, key nerves and their vital functions would have been destroyed. He said in response, "You people amaze me. I nearly kill all of you, then many of you fight your way back to health, and you thank me for saving you!" From early in the recovery I was convinced I would slowly but surely move toward greater health. His response confirmed what I understood deeply, perhaps on a subconscious level. While anesthetized, I connected with death in a new way. It was not time for me to die, but my body had experienced a setback of major proportion.

The doctors and nurses guided me toward healing, and I worked tenaciously to regain what I had lost. But I was never fooled into thinking that I had earned my healing. Each time my body turned a corner, I saw this newfound health as a gift, not an accomplishment. Though sickness and death are an integral part of being human, after experiencing such disability, I have come to see wellness as a priceless gift. I gained great respect for my body as it slowly but surely healed. I was both humbled and exhilarated, as each part of me restored itself. As I fell asleep one night, I felt a nerve tingling in the corner of my mouth; it eventually enabled me to smile on the right side. Each morning I used self-devised eye exercises to help double lines become single again; then two months later I removed my eye patch, looked out the window, and saw winter's individual branches once more. Another night I crossed a twelve-foot-wide hallway without my walker. Several months later I regained enough balance to stand without a walker and give myself a shower. After five months of steady exercise, my eyelids haltingly closed on their own. Six months later I drove my car a short distance by myself at night. Seven months later I began lap swimming again. I now knew that life's setbacks can severely weaken a body, but under certain conditions much of what was lost can be regained.

I was on the receiving end of life for a long time. When we lose what is precious to us, we sometimes accept that we have less control over life than we thought. This acceptance can open us to another dimension of life—its receptive side. The ever-present and deeply human process of controlling, letting go, and then receiving ebbs and flows through our lives. At any given moment each of us is somewhere within this cycle. Through personal experience and that of directees and students, I have noticed that we can focus sometimes more on the controlling aspects and sometimes more on the letting-go aspects of this process. All the while, we miss the dynamics of receiving that have an equivalent value. My body's recovery forced me to give equal weight to receiving. As I recovered, I received gifts more precious than gold. Seeing, hearing, blinking, smiling, bathing, walking, driving, and swimming under my own power were breathtaking gifts. I can never again take life and its vast universe for granted. Contemplating vulnerability humbled me and showed me that everything and everyone is gift. Love choreographs all of us, and when we can no longer dance, vulnerability can remind us that being danced is also great grace.

During the twenty years that have followed my surgery, I have also been understanding, accepting, and adjusting to the irreversible deficits of invasive brain surgery. In Chapter 14 I say more about these lasting deficits, but they are not my focus here. God's gracious response to human frailty is my focus and fascination.

All Shall Be Well

Though gratitude predominated throughout my recovery, there were more difficult times than I have mentioned. Then it was hard to pray because I felt terribly insecure. When my body took turns for the worse, my lack of control frightened me, and praying became impossible. Then Love and her Dance assumed control. I have some understanding of human frailty and the suffering it sparks, but it also mystifies me. The suffering of all creation can confound us. We may quietly ask or anxiously scream, "How can God allow such pain and horror?" Before terrible suffering, you might want to ask me, "How can God possibly change this pain into wellness?"

In the face of deep fragility and its pervasive confusion, I rely on the fourteenth-century mystic, Julian of Norwich. This English mystic was also an anchoress, a known and appreciated ministry during the late medieval period. Anchoresses dedicated themselves to solitude and prayer. Julian lived in a small dwelling attached to a church in the bustling town of Norwich. Since Julian lived a long life, she constantly heard about the terrible plagues, peasant revolts, and the Hundred Years' War that affected the people of Norwich. She had a window that opened onto the street, and from that window she offered guidance to those who sought her help. People traveled great distances to seek the wisdom of this prayerful woman.

Julian wrote only two texts, both called *Showings*. The second is a longer version of the first, and was completed as she matured in her understanding of God's ways. In my own struggle with the previous questions, I was especially drawn to an interaction between Julian and Thomas Merton around God's words, "All shall be well."[2] Julian pleaded for God to help her understand how all things would be well when she heard so much horrible suffering from those who came to her window. She was tenacious when she conversed with Love. Initially God replied to her questioning, "See, I am God. See, I am in all things. See, I do all things. See, I never remove my hands from my works, nor ever shall without end. See, I guide all things to the end that I ordain them for, before time began, with the same power and wisdom and love with which I made them; how should anything be amiss?"[3]

But the longer she listened to her visitors' agony, the more her contemplation involved interrogation of God. Over time the Love of her life responded to this struggle in varied ways. One of God's responses finally calmed her distress and gave her a way of contemplating human pain: "What is impossible to you is not impossible to me. I shall preserve my word in everything, and I shall make everything well."[4] She finally accepted that human beings do not have the capacity to understand the final outcome of human weakness and suffering. What God could do was impossible for her to understand. She could trust, but not comprehend, that every kind of thing would be well.

At the same time God communicated a great deed that God would perform. "This is the great deed which our Lord will do, and in this deed he will preserve his word in everything. And he will make well all which is not well. But what the deed will be and how it will be done, there is no creature who is inferior to Christ who knows it, or will know it until it has been done."[5] God's promise of a great deed that would make all that is not well, well again, brought Julian peace and quieted her questions. Contemplating vulnerability caused her to trust this future great deed, even though she could not understand it.

Nearly six centuries later, in *Conjectures of a Guilty Bystander*, Merton mused about Julian and the great deed God revealed to her. He had been reading *Showings* and was especially impressed with her ability to engage God about her confusion. Merton in interpreting Julian emphasizes that this deed will "not be a deed of destruction and revenge, but of mercy and life, all partial expectations will be exploded and everything will be made right."[6] As he contemplated vulnerability with her under the cedars at his abbey in Kentucky, Merton prayed for the strength to be centered in this secret hope.

Communion: Love's Great Deed

This chapter revolves around God's response and that of everyone else to the severe limitations that followed my brain surgery. Amid Love's multiple ways of comforting or carrying me, I was often aware of creation's interdependence. Frailty forced me to rely on the great deed within which we are all immersed: Love and its communion. Every minute of every day I depended on others' Love for food, baths, medicine, companionship, and so much more. Before my brain surgery, I could have never imagined that God could use great frailty to reveal the powerful interdependence of all things. But after it, while contemplating Love's presence in extreme weakness, I experienced its unimaginable and exquisite Dance.

Love fashions from the frailty of each individual creation a stronger and more infinite harmony of being. God's great deed is already happening; we need only to experience it. We humans have a hard time with interdependence, but contemplating it intensifies our awareness of its harmony. Contemplation refines our vulnerability by slowly and steadily enabling us to see this great deed within which each individual is immersed and to act as if our deep connections matter. Praying with our frailty humbles us, so we can gradually experience with Julian, Merton, and Christ how limitation and communion dance as one.

Do you ever plead to be relieved of suffering or hope that all things are being made right, though you cannot imagine how? Have you ever experienced God and others comforting or carrying you when you needed either or both? When you are distressed I encourage you to interrogate God as boldly as Julian did and to be on the lookout for Love's varied response to your interrogation. If you pay attention with great expectancy, God will surely respond in a time and manner that is most creative for you.

In Chapter 8 I said that vulnerability accepted is spirituality deepened. Here I add that vulnerability accepted is spirituality deepened and expanded – beyond our fondest expectations. Any increase of Love is also spiritual growth, and the reverse is also true. Contemplating your vulnerability will refine your limits by enabling further acceptance of loving communion and the way it holds the finitude of everything and everyone.

Notes

1 Barbara Bradley Hagerty, *Fingerprints of God* (New York: Riverhead Books, 2009), 63–64.

2 Julian of Norwich, *The Showings of Julian of Norwich*, ed. Denise N. Baker (New York: W. W. Norton, 2005), 47.

3 Julian of Norwich, *Julian of Norwich Showings*, trans. Edmund Colledge and James Walsh (New York: Paulist Press, 1978), 199.

4 Julian of Norwich, *Showings*, ed. Baker, 45.

5 Julian of Norwich, *Julian of Norwich*, trans. Colledge and Walsh, 233.

6 Thomas Merton, *Conjectures of a Guilty Bystander* (New York: Doubleday, 1966), 212.

10

Dark Contemplation

Sometimes the light in our lives goes out, and an inner darkness descends, influencing everything. In my late thirties, as I dealt with childhood sexual abuse, darkness invaded all aspects of my life. I had previously experienced life-changing events, but none so intense. This three-year-long walk through hell changed me; dark contemplation transfigures our depth.

Twilight

In my past some struggles in relationships and ministry elicited confusion, anxiety, anger, or fear. The lighter side of life diminished, and I experienced some twilight moments. Many of us experience happenings like these. Whether we are grieving a loss, dealing with personal wounds, or suffering from illness, the joy of life diminishes. Regardless of what triggers life's impasses, milder forms of depression can result from them.

As I contemplate my entire life, only once did life turn pitch black. This was my dark night of the soul. Making it through this experience was not an accomplishment. There is no bragging here; I will never wear this night as a badge of honor. In his book *Dark Nights of the Soul,* Thomas Moore says, "To some, what they think is a dark night may be only a taste of the soul's real darkness, especially if it is relatively quick and easy, and especially if the person experiencing it feels cocky for having gone through it successfully and quickly. The real dark night cannot be dismissed so easily. It leaves a lasting effect and, in fact, alters you for good.

It is nothing to brag about."[1]

A twilight period initiated my nighttime experience, and it came over me when I least expected it. In 1986 I had been elected to the leadership team of the Sisters of Mercy of New Jersey. I assumed responsibility for a process we called Mercy Futures. Seventeen independent communities of sisters were considering becoming one institute. It was a difficult decision for many communities, especially my own, the Sisters of Mercy of New Jersey. Imagine eight thousand women discerning whether each one of their individual communities should let go of its independence so that our mission of mercy would continue. The Sisters of Mercy had been in this decision-making process for a while. Although I didn't know it at the time, I had assumed responsibility for its rockiest period in New Jersey.

As I followed Love's allurement and assumed responsibility for Mercy Futures, I was unaware that its rigors would surface the reality of my sexual abuse. Before this point I believed that what occurred when I was eight had not affected me greatly. Repression can be an amazing mental gift. In order to live my life fully until I had the strength to deal with this evil, repression convinced me that my parents had stopped my abuse before it had damaged me in any way.

I still remember the couch on which I reclined as twilight descended in 1987. We had taken a break from our team meeting, and I was recouping energy for the rest of the meeting. Theresina, our president, and I were always integrating national decision making with our New Jersey process. Since our community was evenly split about forming and joining the institute, and most of us had strong thoughts and feelings on one side or the other, the entire year had been extremely pressured for the rest of the community and me. Coordinating this process had taken more of a toll on me than I understood. As the other team members again joined our facilitator around the table, I had the hardest time rising from the couch. My usual spring was gone.

During the next few weeks an inner heaviness slid over me. One morning during my early swim routine, a strong pull gripped my heart. God, the source of this inner urging, often uses inner attractions to point me in a direction. During this drawing I accepted my need for psychotherapy and even thought of Martha, a therapist that some of my directees visited and valued. By that afternoon Martha and I had scheduled our first appointment. Though I instinctively knew that I needed more help, I also found Love's allurement in this direction irresistible.

Mercy within Mercy within Mercy

Because the depression was intensifying, I also searched for group support. In the beginning I was not particular, and I attended my first Al Anon meeting simply for convenience; it was nearby and on a Friday evening. There the presenter talked about the terrible pain of his childhood abuse, his fall into alcoholism, and his first experience of a "Higher Power." I had gone into that meeting with terrible inner pain; the heaviness had been especially bad that day. As I listened, I felt lighter inside. I had come into the meeting feeling shattered, defective, and alone, and left the meeting feeling companioned in brokenness. Though neither of my parents was an alcoholic, I knew I would attend more of these meetings. I needed to be with people who trusted the impaired aspect of being human and talked openly about a Higher Power. This was home for God and me.

Without realizing it, I was building the support system I would need. What would have seemed inconceivable in previous months was now imperative. I was unknowingly gathering people who could support me for my walk through hell. Life hands many of us impasses that baffle or agonize us. As I took my first steps into the hell of my abuse, I understood that easy and rational solutions would not work. Constance FitzGerald, a Carmelite sister, says that impasse and its powerlessness tempt many people to "give up, to quit, to surrender to cynicism and despair in the face of disappointment, disenchantment, hopelessness, and loss of meaning that encompasses one."[2]

I could not give up or turn to cynicism; that's not my approach to life. In order to come out at the other end with hope restored, I instinctively knew I needed people who could guide and comfort me in the process. For the next five years I would rely on all sorts of professional help: a psychiatrist, medical doctors, group and massage therapists, along with family, friends, and members of twelve-step groups.

Thomas Moore tells his readers to give themselves what they most need when dealing with darkness. "Care rather than cure. Organize your life to support the process. You are incubating your soul, not living a heroic adventure. Arrange life accordingly. Tone it down."[3] In a deep dark night, part of us is dying. It may have taken us a lifetime to develop the part that is dying, so its transformation causes great pain and demands immense energy. "A true dark night of the soul is not a surface challenge but a development that takes you away from the joy of your ordinary life. An external event or an internal mood strikes you at the core of your existence. This is not just a feeling but a rupture in your very being, and it may take a long while to get through to the other end of it."[4]

I now know that dark contemplation, or beholding God in our deepest and darkest recesses, can consume great energy. Then I only knew that my spirit was changing. I had previously experienced some of life's struggles but was more accustomed to an inner buoyancy and optimism. Now my spirit was dull and growing weaker; sadness was spreading throughout my being. Initially I did not understand my malaise, but soon a force welling up from within compelled me to speak about the abuse. During my third session I began sharing it with Martha. Conversation was God's and my first step toward understanding and letting go of the evil within me, but I had no idea this transformation would take several years.

In early November of that year, with the aid of other sisters, I finished coordinating Graced History, the discernment process we used to make our decision about Mercy Futures. Then the depression intensified, forcing me to consider a much-needed break. It was telling me I could no longer juggle innumerable ideas, meetings, plans, and accomplishments; my body and spirit were disabling me. No amount of will power, of which I have plenty, could breach this internal wall. "In a genuine impasse one's accustomed way of acting and living is brought to a standstill. The left side of the brain with its usual application of linear, analytical, conventional thinking is ground to a halt. The impasse forces us to start all over again, driving us to contemplation."[5]

In the past I seldom found decisions difficult. I had often stepped into the unknown with confidence, excitement, and delight. I usually enjoyed newness, and my inner compass often enabled me to create something from scratch. Now everything was radically different. I had no confidence, no inner compass, and was nearly mush inside. The inner compass I still possessed only pointed toward deeper darkness. I told Theresina and the leadership team that I needed a break and had to leave familiar surroundings. I decided to take three weeks, the most I could afford, at a Mercy convent in Philadelphia that was closer to my therapist. I wanted to see my therapist and attend twelve-step meetings more often, all at a much slower pace. Mostly, I would let Love embrace my pain and me.

With my insides in shambles, I had left everything and everyone that was familiar to me for an unfamiliar city and community. I remember my arrival in Philadelphia well. I stopped to eat before going to the convent. As I ate, I cried quietly, but inside I was howling. I was lost inwardly and outwardly. I felt like a blind person trying to cross a busy intersection without a single aid. FitzGerald says that a sense of aloneness is intrinsic to dark nights. "At the deepest levels of impasse, one sees the support systems on which one had depended pulled out from under one and asks if anything, if anyone, is trustworthy."[6] Though I had support from friends, I experienced profound aloneness, because they could not touch the depth of this pain or my growing sense of being lost. I did not know what I or anyone could do to rid me of this intensifying gloom.

As I continued eating, I silently but intently cried out to God for relief and some direction. In the midst of my pleading, I sensed Love's presence. Not with words but with an inner strength, God let me know he was not lost. I did not feel strong, but I did feel his strength and sensed Love would guide me through this intense darkness. Then God asked me to take only the next step—to go to the convent. That was a relief, because I thought I could do that. As I left the restaurant Love held my spirit and enabled me to take the next step. Sheer powerlessness before the impasse of my abuse was surfacing. So was the darkness of the human condition.

That night I felt welcomed to Philadelphia by a small community of sisters. For those few weeks I experienced friendliness, freedom, and safety in their community. I will always be grateful to the Sisters of Mercy in Philadelphia who were so merciful without knowing the hell I was experiencing.

My therapist and I began to meet twice a week, and I attended twelve-step meetings more frequently. I was feeling my way with these meetings and finally found an Incest Survivors' Anonymous meeting that felt right to me. I found great comfort in my attendance at twelve-step meetings. Mercy came in varying sizes and shapes during that time. Listening to others share the pain of their abuse and the benefit they found in recovery drew me into my own process more deeply. During those meetings I learned that I desperately needed to be in conversation with others who knew the same darkness.

Every time I needed something new to enable my healing or just to sustain me in its rigors, something appeared. I was learning a great deal about the providence of God and the wisdom of the universe's Dance. Thomas Merton talks about "mercy within mercy within mercy."[7] As I write about this dark night I can now see Mercy's Dance throughout the darkness. Then it was nearly invisible; night blinded me.

Night

During this Philadelphia retreat, twilight became night. "During the dark night there is no choice but to surrender control, give in to unknowing, and stop and listen to whatever signals of wisdom might come along. It's a time of enforced retreat and perhaps unwilling withdrawal. The dark night is more than a learning experience; it's a profound initiation into a realm that nothing in the culture, so occupied with external concerns and material success, prepares you for."[8]

While in Philadelphia the horror of my abuse became more evident to me. Attending meetings, listening to the stories of others, sharing everything in therapy and spiritual direction, and exposing it all to the Love of my life dissolved any repression that remained. What were distant memories became relived experiences. The details returned full force.

When I shared my abuse with Martha in our third therapy session, I immediately realized there was a missing piece. Most of my memories were intact, but as an adult I had never realized that there was a conscious hole in one set of memories. The events that surrounded this missing piece were what most terrified me as a child and intensified my agony as an adult.

My father enjoys collecting stamps and coins. One of life's terrible paradoxes for him and me was that one of his great enjoyments played a role in my abuse. My father had an elderly close friend whom my brothers and I called "Aunty." She had been a close friend of my grandmother's and baby-sat my father when he was young. Once he reached adulthood they gradually became friends. As that friendship deepened, so did their trust in each other.

Her husband, Gus, was an elderly man with a fine stamp collection. He and my father attended stamp meetings and exhibitions together, and my father learned more about collecting stamps from him. Both of them thought I could learn something valuable about stamp collecting from Gus. I began an elementary approach to stamp collecting when I was around eight. I would stop at his house on my way home from school and walk the short distance to our house afterwards.

His abuse of me began during our first stamp-collecting session. From the beginning he would fondle my genitals as I sat in his lap at the desk. That he could fondle my genitals with one hand, arrange and rearrange stamps with the other, and talk about the origin of each stamp all at the same time only accentuates his illness. This continued for a few visits. We had anywhere from four to six visits before his disease worsened.

The basement of their house was where most of this occurred. For me as a child it seemed like a large room, and his desk was in the furthest left corner from the entrance. Except for a small desk lamp and the meager light that filtered through three tiny basement windows, we were surrounded by near darkness. The darkness was part of his sickness. In the kitchen above us we heard his wife's movement as she prepared supper. If he ever heard her coming down the steps, he could quickly remove his hand from my pants, rearrange my clothing, and conceal his evil acts. The secretive nature of child molestation only intensifies the terribly destructive power of this illness.

From the beginning he had been prompting me not to tell my parents or anyone about his sideline to stamp collecting. Thank God, I no longer remember any particular words he whispered in my ear. All of them discouraged me from sharing our "special secret" with anyone. If I told my parents it would supposedly ruin the special connection between him and me. His whispers had a rarefied tone to them. As I look back, he seemed to experience something extraordinary through this fondling. His fondling and his messages about secrets were extremely confusing. I had no reason to hide anything from my parents, so the fondling and messages disturbed me. For a while I obeyed his requests for secrecy. He was an adult, and up to that point I had trusted adults, especially my parents.

These words confused me only for a while. His controlling messages fell apart one afternoon when Aunty was not in the house. Now I know that the horror of his illness progressed rapidly as soon as the possibility of detection was minimized. Gus and I sat in the living room for the first time. I suspect this was the easiest place for him to get me into a reclining position. I had just recovered from the chicken pox. As we sat on separate chairs, he feigned concern. I say "feigned" because this manipulative masquerade infuriates me as an adult. I also say "feigned" because even as a child, I sensed this "concern" was not genuine. It felt different from the concern of my parents and the other adults in my life. I do not know how aware he was of his pretense. I only know my experience of it, and that is more than enough. His illness surely prevented him from seeing how damaging his actions were toward me.

Most of the marks that the chicken pox had left were of no interest to him. He was interested in my genitals only. I no longer remember the conversation that led to the question, "Do you have chicken pox marks on your genitals?" Nor do I remember the word he used to talk about my genitals. Whatever it was, I understood the question, and in all innocence responded truthfully, "Yes."

As he spoke, he played the role of caring nurse. He would have to examine them to be sure they would not become harmful to me. I no longer remember the rationale he used to get me onto the couch and naked from the waist down. I clearly remember him sitting on the couch between my legs, pretending to examine with great care the marks that the chicken pox had left, while he gaped at and groped my genitals.

As I shared this part of my abuse with my therapist, I realized that I had a massive and pronounced hole in my memory. I did not remember how I rose from the couch, dressed myself, or walked home. I had no recollection of anything that happened between the time when he manipulated my genitals, and when I sat at our kitchen table getting ready to tell my mother a day or so later. The before and after memories were vivid; the in-between memories were nonexistent.

In therapy I realized I had dissociated from part of the abuse—the part with which I could least cope. As I began to deal with my abuse, I knew that Gus had raped me with his fingers and eyes, but I did not know what had occurred while I was still on the couch in a state of dissociation. Throughout my recovery I was plagued with the possibility that he had also raped or tried to rape me with his penis. These last abusive acts evoked agony throughout this dark time. My greatest suffering during those years revolved around that event. The actions that I knew, and those that I did not know, had a torment all their own. Whenever God and I were most intimate during my healing, it was always related to the last aspect of my abuse.

Once I realized, as an adult, that the abuse had affected me deeply, I began to talk with my parents about it. I had remembered some of what happened a day or two after that last abusive act. As a child, while sitting at our kitchen table, I realized that I no longer wanted to collect stamps and told my mother that Gus was "putting his hands in my pants." As an adult I remembered little of that conversation, but knew my mother had talked with my father, and both of them made sure I never saw Gus again.

While recovering, my parents shared some details I never knew. They had talked with Aunty first, and then she confronted Gus about the abuse I had shared with my mother. He acknowledged that he had fondled my genitals, and soon after went into hiding for a few weeks. My parents assumed he was afraid of prosecution. They had decided not to prosecute because they thought it would harm me more. Gus eventually returned home, became sick, and died a few years later.

During my recovery from sexual abuse, I listened to many survivor stories. I soon realized that my experience was different in two ways. As a child I trusted my parents enough to tell them I was being abused. When I told them, they believed me, confronted my abuser, stopped the abuse, and never blamed me. Many of the survivors I listened to had not been able to tell their parents, or when they did, they were not believed. In most of these cases, they then endured prolonged abuse. All abuse is horrendously destructive. Long-term abuse has its own hell.

As an adult I was grateful to discover that when my brothers reached young adulthood my father had told them about my abuse. I was thankful that he cared enough about me and my abuse to tell them. As I look back on my parents' response, I am eternally grateful. Without their quick and strong response on my behalf, the abuse would have worsened, I might not have survived childhood, or recovery as an adult might have been impossible.

I had hoped the pain would diminish during my three weeks of hard work in Philadelphia, but as I returned to New Jersey, I was petrified. My companions were sheer darkness, and a God who was inviting me to accept it more deeply. Mercy Futures and the stress it was evoking in a number of Mercy communities, including mine, added to my inner turmoil. I had no clue about how I would handle leadership responsibilities along with deep inner upheaval.

Even though God and I were dancing together, it was to an agonizing inner music. The return was aggravated by my realization that I had no idea how long this healing would take. I had accepted the reality that Love wanted to heal all of me, each physical inch and every emotional expanse. Since God is the healer par excellence, I had given him the control. Once I accepted the darkness, letting go of the reins was all I could do. Love would have to lead this Dance, its timing and its movement; that is the nature of dark contemplation. As I drove home I took the next step—barely.

Notes

1 Thomas Moore, *Dark Nights of the Soul* (New York: Gotham Books, 2004), xix.

2 Constance FitzGerald, "Impasse and the Dark Night," in *Women's Spirituality: Resources for Christian Development*, ed. Joanne Wolski Conn (New York: Paulist Press, 1996), 411.

3 Moore, *Dark Nights*, xx.

4 Ibid., xiv.

5 Conn, *Women's Spirituality*, 412.

6 Ibid.

7 Thomas Merton, *The Intimate Merton*, ed. Patrick Hart and Jonathan Montaldo (San Francisco: Harper San Francisco, 1999), 102.

8 Moore, *Dark Nights*, xviii.

11

Suffering Transfigured

Dark contemplation creates a beyond-belief awareness of Love and its ways. When someone stays close to us as we stagger through hell, we cannot forget this Love, because it sears itself into our consciousness. This Love has convinced me that it holds everything and everyone, especially when we are most weak and life most bleak. In Thomas Moore's words, "You don't choose a dark night for yourself. It is given to you. Your job is to get close enough to it and sift for its gold."[1] Though I did not know it at the time, I was panning for and actually finding gold. Dark contemplation transfigures us. It helps us trust a Love that is strong enough to change death into resurrection.

Midnight

As I became utterly present to the pain of my abuse and the darkness it created within me, midnight arrived. This, the gravest part of the healing, may have lasted for a year or so. Without my many support systems, I do not know how I could have made it through this year.

On my return to New Jersey, I continued to receive therapy and spiritual direction, and to attend many incest survivor meetings. Early in these meetings I began to notice that many women and a few men would talk about an "inner child." Their inner children were deeply real to them; they bore the scars of their abuse and were central to their healing process. Initially, I was unsure about this "inner child" thing; my skeptic saw it as a gimmick. But they were so sincere, and their stories so genuine, that I stayed open to the possibility that I might experience a similar presence. Before long I was talking about and relating to my inner child. My abuse, especially its last episode, was extremely difficult for me as a child. Once I reconnected deeply with that part of my life, I was shocked to find a child who was near death.

All of the pain and destruction of that event roared to the surface. I relived those heinous and ungodly moments of my childhood. God drew me into them in order to transform their destructive power, but it was a costly transformation for both of us. I will never know the precise connection between my walk through hell and the brain tumor that was found six months after night had ended. My spirit withstood hell well; perhaps my body lacked the same agility.

Year-long midnight is treacherous. How I got through it without more damage, I will never know. Love alone is the reason I made it through rape as a child, and through the power of its continuous destruction as an adult. During that year prayer was like the air I breathed; without it I would die in minutes. I was one of the living dead walking through my days. Thankfully I slept well each night, because sleep and prayer were a much-needed relief from the evil that God was transforming all too slowly.

Before this suffering I prayed in a more fluid manner and seldom scheduled personal prayer, but slogging through this dark night compelled me to schedule prayer. An hour of daily personal prayer enabled me to wake up, get out of bed, and walk through my day. After community prayer and a parish liturgy, I often sat in church for an hour of prayer. God and I were quietly intimate then. During that hour I experienced none of the heaviness of depression, evil of rape, or darkness of spirit. Love gently filled my torso and a calm spread throughout my body. For that hour I soaked in all the peace and Love I could, because every day as I rose to leave, walked through the church door, and my foot left the church step and hit the pavement, depression and darkness flooded me again. It would last until I fell asleep that night. My ministerial responsibilities would distract me somewhat from the turmoil, especially when I offered someone spiritual guidance. Believe me, I took advantage of every distraction I could find, but the darkness was close by, no matter how enjoyable the distraction.

A few of the women in my Incest Survivor groups brought teddy bears to the meetings. The women would carry these companions into the meetings in brown paper bags and then hold them while they listened and shared. Like the "inner child thing," I found this a little strange.

Then one day I felt compelled to find a stuffed bear for myself. It was Holy Thursday and I was in more pain than usual. My therapy appointment was still a week away, and my survivors' meeting a few days away. I needed something to sustain me through that day's pain and darkness. I had already prayed; more prayer would not cut it. Suddenly I needed a teddy bear.

My inner abused child was exceedingly present by this point and needed a cuddly bear. I began my search for a bear that was large enough to hold but small enough to carry, soft enough to comfort but firm enough to embrace, cute enough to befriend without being sentimental. I knew just what I wanted and found it sooner than I thought possible. It was brown, sixteen inches long, very soft, with a wonderfully caring expression. Its expression hooked me, and I bought it immediately.

Whenever I hugged this bear, the intensity of the pain soothed a bit, and this was both surprising and amazing. I cannot explain this phenomenon; I only know it worked. During this period I used anything that soothed the pain without damaging me in other ways.

I decided not to hide my bear in a paper bag. I carried it proudly to therapy sessions and twelve-step meetings along public walkways and streets. Love me, love my bear was my philosophy. This inanimate creature was helping me heal. It had gained my respect, and there was no way I was going to hide it in a paper bag. Besides, it was cute and had too much personality to be hidden in a bag. One of my nieces now has this cuddly creature. When I notice it now, it no longer has the same hold on me, but it gently reminds me of that extremely difficult time, and the Love that carried me through it.

A Most Tender Dance

Writing about the details of my abuse is easier than describing Love's response to my injuries. Once in a group that I led a man balked at the idea of sharing what happened in prayer: "I would share aspects of my sex life with others before I would share my prayer, and I'm not going to share anything about my sex life!" This statement underscores how both prayer and sexuality arise from the deepest and most intimate parts of us.

Thus it is difficult to write publicly about God's response to my sexual abuse and its damage. Still, I know Love is asking me to be as open as I can. Often, so very often, when I prayed quietly each morning, Love was simply present within me, soothing and strengthening me in whatever way I most needed. Many times this loving presence moved tenderly and in prolonged ways around my heart and throughout my sexual organs. I gradually realized that God was determined to soothe each and every physical inch that Gus had abused.

Years of deepening familiarity with Love's stirring made me even more sensitive to this most tender dynamic. This gentle migration of Love throughout my body had a power of its own; it knew when, where, and how I needed to be touched interiorly. It drifted ever so slowly through all parts of me that had been abused. All of the sexual and emotional parts of me needed the most delicate affection for a long time. Love caressed me this way on an "as needed" basis for three or four years.

Tenderness itself also embraced the child within me. The more this child was cradled and soothed by this affectionate, inner Dance, the stronger she and I became. My child's shift from near death to greater health was gradual and ever so slow. When God wanted to heal me as an adult, the masculine dimension of God became apparent, and when Love wished to soothe my inner child, I sensed the feminine dimension of God. On one of my retreats Jim, my spiritual director, gave me a beautiful picture of Mary holding the infant Jesus. The picture radiated delicate and strong Love. I prayed with this picture throughout the retreat, and the feminine dimension of God took over whenever I did. She held, soothed, cuddled, loved, and healed this near lifeless child. Throughout this healing process my inner child was imperceptibly transformed. At one point I would sense a speck of animation in her, at another point, a smile or bit of joy. The Mother caressed, nuzzled, and held her close again and again.

God's Dance was simple, unhurried, continuous, and steady. All of my human support systems helped greatly in my healing. But God alone had the capacity to touch my inmost self. While I contemplated Love to the best of my ability, it was transforming every damaged part of me. Both as a Mother and as an intimate masculine Spouse, Love was healing me with utmost sensitivity. It soothed and revived me in ways that no person could, but there was another side to this tender Dance.

Though I had a superb support system that helped me follow Love's lead into the most broken part of my being, I must single out Louise Gorka, a friend and a Sister of Mercy. She is especially sensitive to Love's presence in the joy and pain of her life, and this enables her to see the same in others. She also has a refined ability to follow the movement of God. Louise joined me in my deepest pain and fear at crucial points in my recovery; her presence helped me stay closer to the Love moving in me.

Louise's presence was crucial during a particular aspect of my healing from sexual abuse. The healing of my body, emotions, and inner child all supported my recovery. But God also confronted and dispersed the evil that my abuser spewed into my body and being. I have been dealing with fibromyalgia since I was twenty-seven. This disease primarily affects women, and doctors do not know its cause or have a cure. Since the pain of my fibromyalgia was still out of control at that point in my life, I experienced intense pain in my lower back whenever I sat for longer than ten minutes. So one time when I had asked Louise for spiritual direction, I had to lie on the living-room couch in order to relieve this pressure and pain. Little did I realize that Love would use this prone position to confront and overcome evil.

I no longer remember how this spiritual direction began, but quickly I became aware of a darkness that was radically different from everything previously experienced. It was black, impenetrable, and ominous. I felt its presence enter my body through my vagina, spread throughout my body, leave through my head, and then encapsulate me in itself. There was more to the experience than this, and I am very glad I have forgotten the details. It was all quite frightening, and I could never have stayed present to the dynamic without Louise's support. Since she had more objectivity than I, she sensed Love's presence in the midst of evil better than I. Thus she had an ability to stay present to God even while attending to evil. Her courage and strength enabled mine.

There I was as an adult, in prayer, encapsulated in a black viscous material that I knew was evil. I sensed that evil had in some way affected me during the last abusive episode. Now I was utterly powerless before its strength, as I had been as a child. I had sufficient strength to pray, but I cannot imagine that I would have trusted prayer as deeply had I been alone. Before I knew it, a soft, subtle, potent, and tenacious light began moving around me, gradually replacing the blackened capsule with itself. Then it moved in an opposing direction to the viscous substance. It entered my body through my head, traveled gently and gradually throughout my torso, and stayed longer in my abdomen.

Light gently overcame the black substance, which seemed impervious and all-powerful to me, but before this gentle light it was impotent and frail. In my early periods of recovery, I did not yet grasp a connection between evil and this last abusive act. Now Love revealed to me that it was destroying the evil I had internalized as a child and that was still influencing me as an adult. Thankfully I caught Love's transformation of the evil!

Dawn

Since I returned to Philadelphia every other week to see my therapist, I often walked along Philadelphia's Schuylkill River before again returning to New Jersey. This had become a three-year-long ritual. After those sessions, I needed time to pray, so I meandered regardless of the weather. While strolling one spring day, the dark night that had lasted three long years shifted. I have forgotten the details that preceded this quantum leap, but I do recall asking Love about my dissociation. Would I ever know all that was done to my body while my mind traveled elsewhere? Would my child be healed?

Suddenly I experienced a simple but bright explosion of light deep within me. Then Love spoke: "You need to know nothing more about that incident; it is more than you need to bear." A strong protective tone accompanied these words. Since I seldom hear "words" in my prayer, they embedded themselves in my memory and freed me. Throughout my recovery I had wanted to know what Gus did during my dissociation, but Love's words were gentle and firm, and my unceasing need to know everything vanished. This liberation brought its own relief to the recovery process. Then I sensed the presence of my child holding my hand and skipping joyfully beside me. During the long healing process she had moved from near death, to some health, and was now bursting with life, joy, and freedom.

My shift from midnight to dawn began abruptly with this prayer by the Schuylkill. But I did not realize this immediately, because my everyday distractions made the reversal seem more gradual. This inner burst of light and my skipping child stayed with me, but I was quite busy at that point in my life. I had made the difficult decision to take my name out of consideration for another four-year term of community leadership. God and I knew how draining my current four-year term, the Mercy Futures' process, and all the darkness they evoked, had been. I needed a rest from positional leadership.

So that spring I was in transition. The search for a new ministry while completing the current one somewhat distracted me from the healing process. But one day several weeks after light's interior burst, while driving in New Jersey, I recognized a lightheartedness that I had missed for three years. I began to appreciate the normal ups and downs of life from an interior levity rather than darkness.

Noonday

I ended my leadership term in June of 1990. In September I moved to Philadelphia and began a new ministry at Chestnut Hill College. Two weeks later I was told I had a benign brain tumor that would gradually kill me unless it was removed. The early chapters tell the story of this operation and of never-ending Love.

How could I have imagined that Love would use serious brain surgery to end my journey through darkness and bring me into noonday light? While trudging through hell, Love was transforming me, but it is hard to grasp what is happening while in darkness. All I did was surrender to the Dance; that took all I had to give. Dark contemplation consumes our minds, hearts, and flesh, so I took only one step at a time, to the best of my ability.

During dark contemplation we are undone, and during the most severe darkness we become mush inside. This undoing elicits pain, but our spiritual self is renewing us. While we suffer, a mysterious part of us that is both God and our deepest self can be terribly creative. All the skills we have developed to achieve great things are useless in this darkness. There are no skills that prepare us for suffering through a muddled and dark chrysalis. Thomas Moore says of the dark night, "Don't try to have it finished. Don't try to figure it out. Don't try to outsmart it. You wouldn't interfere with the natural birth process, so don't fidget your way into the journey of soul that will make you more of a person and reveal your destiny."[2]

While contemplating darkness, I could no longer proceed with the more common, meeting-filled life of my previous years. My dark night had unraveled my "heroic" self, the one who did three years' work during my first year on the leadership team. Moore says: "It helps to regularly undo the hard-won ego development, to unravel the self and culture you have woven over the years. The night sea journey takes you back to your primordial self, not the heroic self that burns out and falls to judgment, but to your original self, your greater and deeper being."[3]

I now see this terribly painful period as the *most* profoundly creative period of my life. Then I only knew I was falling apart. During those three years I learned so much about the creativity of our spiritual self and its capacity to contemplate darkness. The Love that moves deeply throughout the universe, and moved within me during that period, had a radically different approach to creativity than I did. It had little need for the heroics of great achievements; it cherished mush. All too slowly Love created incredible light from nearly overwhelming darkness. When we contemplate darkness deeply and for a long time, Love takes hell and makes heaven.

Since that dark period, I have rethought all of my former assumptions about sadness, despair, and emptiness. I no longer see them as temporary and unavoidable detours from the more "normal" life of meetings, social commitments, and productivity. I now see these experiences and all aspects of dark contemplation as integral parts of a healthy and happy life. Without them there is no deepening spirituality and the unfathomable peace and joy that accompany it.

Love Suffers, Dies, and Rises in Us

Dark contemplation exposes pure Love. Because human beings have little control during times of great suffering, our pain can force us to surrender to a Love that moves within our suffering. When we glimpse God staying close to us and staggering through hell with us, these sightings sear Love unto death into our consciousness. We gradually experience flawless, limitless, and unconditional Love. Repeated experiences of such magnanimity, especially of Love unto death, empower us to love others similarly.

While walking through my own darkness, I knew God was agonizing with me. We were one in suffering, but this union offered me little relief. Only after I awoke from anesthesia did I realize what God had done. *The depth to which I let God carry me into my darkness influenced the height to which we rose into light and Love.* Though I was slowly healed of abuse's evil, it was the Love that

I awakened to that most transformed me. Now I am preoccupied with and must write about a Love that suffers, dies, and rises with us, whether or not we are aware. Great-hearted Love transforms our Love and enables our Dance. Chapters 2 and 3 describe my ongoing experience of this incredible Dance.

If you are struggling through a dark time, whether because of illness, loss, addiction, or whatever, ask and even beg to experience the unconditional Love that surrounds and fills us. Ask to trust the Dance that is suffering and dying with you and will also rise with you. Do not give up on your entreaties, because God is especially sensitive to our pleading. But do know that God knows how to heal and transform you, and Love's timing is far wiser than ours.

Ask to trust that Love is holding you in your agony, even if you do not experience it. Implore even when you cannot see, because reaching out is of the essence in dark contemplation. Then when you least expect it, God may transfigure your suffering, and you may experience the Dance. But when it comes to contemplating God's presence, especially in darkness, we are all novices. We too easily concentrate on the mist of our lives and miss the sun. Try to remember that, in Merton's words, Love sees you as someone who is walking around "shining like the sun."

Notes

1 Thomas Moore, *Dark Nights of the Soul* (New York: Gotham Books, 2004), xv.

2 Ibid., 13.

3 Ibid., 5.

12

Contemplating Injustice

My awareness of Love's presence in the darkness of large-scale persecution came gradually. It began when four women were assassinated in El Salvador in 1980. In this chapter we see how God uses the life, death, and resurrection of Maura Clarke, Jean Donovan, Ita Ford, and Dorothy Kazel to proclaim that God transforms evil into goodness in her own time frame. They expose a Cosmic Dance that suffers, dies, and rises in all creation. In societal dark nights we meet a most rarefied Love.

Love unto Death

As I sat alone at the breakfast table perusing the front page of the *Boston Globe,*[1] a picture on the bottom of the page drew me. Three Maryknoll Sisters were kneeling and praying over the lifeless bodies of Maryknoll Sisters Maura Clarke and Ita Ford, lay missionary Jean Donovan, and Ursuline Sister Dorothy Kazel. Sections of their dirty, bloated, and lifeless bodies were partially covered with tree branches.

As I gazed at the picture, I saw absolute goodness and sheer evil and felt inexpressible rage at whoever ordered the rape and murder of women whose only crime was their support of El Salvador's poor. That picture gripped me, but it took years before I understood its impact. Then I had no idea it was evoking my contemplation of God's movement in societal dark nights and the injustice that causes them. On the surface I was moved and appalled. Deeper still, Love was developing a just heart.

On December 2, 1980, Jean and Dorothy went to the El Salvador airport to pick up Ita and Maura from their 6 p.m. flight. Dorothy, Jean, Ita, and Maura never returned home. When it became clear that the four women were missing, Paul Schindler, a Roman Catholic priest and the pastor of the Cleveland missionary team in El Salvador, reported this to Ambassador Thomas White at the U.S. Embassy in El Salvador. Ambassador White immediately requested the assistance of Defense Minister Garcia in finding the missionaries. The Salvadoran minister promised full cooperation.

On December 3, Father Schindler reported that local people had found the women's empty and charred parish van off the highway. The next morning another church official called Ambassador White to say that the bodies had been found on a nearby farm in a shallow grave. White, Patricia Lasbury, the U.S. consul, and some sisters arrived soon to exhume and identify their bodies. Ambassador White had the disinterment videotaped.[2]

An extensive cover-up by Salvadoran military leaders stalled the investigation of their murders. Several years later five members of the National Guard were arrested, and a few of them shared more about the events of that night. Deputy Sergeant Luis Colindres Aleman, the officer in charge of the National Guard detachment involved, ordered his men to set up a roadblock on the highway from the airport. They let all other vehicles pass but stopped the women's van and took charge of the vehicle. Once or twice during the next few hours Colindres would leave the group to make phone calls.

The women's bodies tell us all we need to know about this part of the story. Since Jean's and Ita's bodies were badly bruised, they may have been beaten. Then, at the end of a lonely dirt road, these four unarmed women were tormented, raped, and murdered in execution style by members of El Salvador's military.

I have saved that *Boston Globe* photograph since 1980, and those women have become part of my prayer and life. Contemplating them happens spontaneously. When I invite students to contemplate them and then listen to their prayer, I sometimes cry. Though I try to control these tears, they have a power of their own. At first the strength of this tearful response baffled me, but slowly I realized I was beholding God's Love unto death. While praying, I behold God, the four women, and great-hearted Love. I feel the pain that can accompany any suffering, but mostly I experience Love, a crucified and resurrected Love moving through me. Tears are my only response before the magnanimity of these women and God.

Contemplation changes us in unimaginable ways, so it can be dangerous. At one point these women were outside the scope of my awareness; then they became part of my heart. Contemplation makes siblings out of strangers.

Great-hearted Love

Those women's lives are as compelling as their final photograph and as arresting today as they were in the 1980s. How did their lives lead to such an appalling end in the darkness of December 2, 1980? Dorothy Kazel was the only sister who had been in El Salvador for some time, ministering there since 1974. At the time of their murder, Jean Donovan had been there for one and a half years, Ita Ford for six months, and Maura Clarke for only three months.

These women were not high-profile political or church leaders nor were they guerrillas or secret agents for anyone, as some Salvadoran and U.S. politicians claimed. They were missionaries of faith, hope, and charity. They brought Love and the Word of God to sick, starving, and homeless refugees who were fleeing the war in sections of their country. Their actions reveal their deep commitment to Jesus' words, "Blessed are you who are poor, for the kingdom of God is yours," and "Blessed are you who are now hungry, for you will be satisfied."[3]

Dorothy Kazel was a member of the religious congregation of Ursuline Sisters of Cleveland. In 1974 she had joined the church team from there that was ministering to the people of El Salvador. While she visited homes and prepared people to receive the sacraments, she also witnessed the terrible poverty of the majority. By the late 1970s, as El Salvador's violence escalated over its horrendous economic injustice, she was taking many new homeless people to refugee centers. In a letter home she said El Salvador was a country "writhing in pain—a country that daily faces the loss of so many of its people—and yet a country that is waiting, hoping, yearning for peace. . . . Our leaders have to continue preaching the Word of the Lord even though it may mean 'laying down your life' in a very real sense."[4]

Jean Donovan joined Dorothy in 1979. At the age of twenty-seven, she was the youngest of the four. She had grown up in Westport, Connecticut. While studying for a business degree in Cleveland, she volunteered at the diocesan youth ministry office and heard about the diocese's mission to El Salvador. She experienced "a gut feeling" about going to El Salvador. "I want to get closer to [God], and that's the only way I think I can." After receiving training as a missionary, she arrived in El Salvador in July 1979. There she was the diocesan Caritas coordinator, providing food for the poor and refugees.

For three years in his Sunday homilies Oscar Romero, El Salvador's archbishop, spotlighted the country's massive economic inequity, the murders of priests, and the military's brutality; finally, his bold preaching was too threatening for the military and its death squads, and he was assassinated on March 24, 1980. Dorothy and Jean took turns keeping vigil at his bier. Both of them understood the danger they were now in. Jean wrote to a friend, "Several times I have decided to leave El Salvador. I almost could except for the children, the poor bruised victims of this insanity. Who would care for them? Whose heart would be so staunch as to favor the reasonable thing in a sea of their tears and helplessness? Not mine, dear friend, not mine."[5]

Born in Brooklyn, New York, Ita Ford worked a number of years as a book editor at Sadlier and Co. and then joined the Maryknoll Sisters. After six years of missionary experience in Chile, she joined another Maryknoll friend, Carla Piette, in El Salvador about six months before her death. When her friend Carla drowned several months later in a swollen river they were crossing, Ita was alone in her ministry. Maura Clarke, another Maryknoll sister, joined her in late August 1980.

Maura wrote, "We have the refugees, women and children, outside the door and some of their stories are incredible. What is happening here is all so impossible, but happening. The endurance of the poor and their faith through this terrible pain is constantly pulling me to a deeper faith response."[6] Both Maryknoll sisters lived in the parish church complex at the end of a dirt highway two hours north of San Salvador. Within that impoverished complex were small storerooms, makeshift bathing facilities, and a loft. Each of the sisters lived in her own small, bare storeroom. Refugees often slept in the loft.

These four women were at the epicenter of El Salvador's intensifying civil war and they knew it. The violence forced them to fall back on a faith that revealed to them a God who is crucified daily in the lives of the poor. Their loving fidelity led to their own crucifixion in dirt and darkness. We see Love move forcefully in those who confront injustice; Dorothy, Jean, Ita, and Maura reveal this might with their very lives.

"Christ Is My Life"

The published letters of Ita Ford reveal much about these women's love of God and God's poor people. In them we read about the ups and downs of Ita's spiritual growth and her walk through El Salvador's hell. We also glimpse Love's presence in that country's darkness.

Approximately one month after Ita and Carla Piette arrived in El Salvador, they were asked by Bishop Rivera Damas to minister to the people of Chalatenango. Because the guerrilla movement was very strong in this northern province, it was an exceptionally dangerous area. But people with enormous humanitarian needs were fleeing the area, so it was a high priority for the church. The diocese of San Salvador was getting ready to supply Chalatenango with food, medicine, and refugee centers, and Ita and Carla would be the diocesan channels for this service.

These women knew that their journey with the poor endangered their lives. With friends, Carla teased about dyeing her hair blond, because the armed forces did not kill blond, blue-eyed North Americans. In June 1980 Ita wrote in a letter to two other Maryknoll sisters, "My baptism into the violence was spontaneously arranged by some local thugs (I'd guess thirteen or fourteen years old) as we were coming in one evening around 7 p.m. Coming up behind me, one put a knife to my ribs, another a machete to my neck. Being New York City trained, I said, 'I'm a nun. I won't hurt you.' [B]ecause a truck was passing by they got scared [and ran away]."[7] Although they took her bag and watch, they left her unharmed.

Carla and she "had talked lots of times about the possibility of our dying because of things here being very violent."[8] In early October she wrote to her mother and said the last few days had been tough. The seminary and chancery were bombed, and a member of the Human Rights Commission and another priest had been killed. "That probably makes more news than all the 'beat up' who die. Who are many. Someone remarked the other day that all our conversations are about death. It's probably true, because it's all around and often so barbaric."[9]

After being there for two months she wrote to her sister, Rene Ford Sullivan: "I'm taking the day off today to be alone, to think. I'm super saturated with horror stories and daily body counts to the point that I thought I'd hit the next person who told me that someone else was killed. I'm not sure how you get 'acclimated' to a country that has an undeclared civil war going. . . . There're a lot of bizarre things that go on in this country including the help from Uncle Sam. It's pathetic that there're millions for army equipment, but nothing for humanitarian help until war is declared."[10]

El Salvador was riddled with murderous chaos, so there was nothing predictable or well planned about Ita's ministry and prayer. Nonetheless, she engaged her confusing and violent reality. Her ability to face El Salvador's horror and share her struggles with others illumines her spiritual depth. One letter to her mother is especially poignant. Her close friend Carla had died only three weeks before when their Jeep turned over while they were crossing a flooding stream. Carla had pushed Ita from the Jeep and the swollen river separated them. Ita survived, but

Carla drowned.

Ita was responding to her mother's fears for her safety. She shares her confusion about her reasons for remaining in El Salvador. "I truly believe I should be here, and I can't even tell you why. A couple of weeks ago Carla and I were praying and we both cried because it was so unclear to us why we were here, although we felt strongly that we should be."[11]

Constance FitzGerald, the Carmelite sister I introduced in Chapter 10, says darkness places us on a "path into the unknown, into the uncontrolled and unpredictable margins of life."[12] As Carla and Ita, and then Maura and Ita, prayed together, they were breaking away from typical responses to possible danger; reason, analysis, and planning ceased to be their primary response to El Salvador's darkness. Acknowledging their powerlessness before massive violence, they relied on deeper, more contemplative processes.

In the same letter to her mother, Ita said, "All I can share with you is God's palpable presence has never been more real ever since we came to Salvador. He's made a lot of things clear to us. What we should be doing, etc. I trust in that and hope you can too."[13] It is hard to walk through darkness, and impossible without strength of soul. But I understand how the palpable presence of which they speak enabled them to move through that horrendous darkness.

In the midst of unbelievable societal agony, these four women were accepting the sorrow and powerlessness of finitude and surrendering these experiences to mystery. FitzGerald explains aspects of yielding: "*If* one can yield in the right way, responding with *full consciousness* of one's suffering in the impasse yet daring to believe that new possibilities can be given, then one will have the capacity to receive the future, whatever its hue."[14] Ita's yielding to mystery comes through in simple lines. "On the whole, God has been very good. We still seem to be fairly well glued together in spite of the daily horrors."[15] In longer passages, like the following, one can hear her let go of the need for control and predictability, and then notice Christ's response to her surrender. "Phil, 1:21: 'For me, Christ is my life'—As usual the scripture is not only appropriate, but right to the point, not just that Christ is the Lord of Life, in charge of the day and the hour, something which has to be thought about in this country of forty to fifty and sometimes a hundred assassinations a day, but that he is the meaning all along the way and in the fullness. His kingdom of brotherhood, justice, peace, and love is what my life is given to—right now, here in Salvador."[16]

Ita contemplated Love's movement in El Salvador's horror. Her surrender to mystery was clearer in a letter she wrote her Maryknoll sisters and friends in Chile a few weeks after Carla's death. She was missing the way sisters gather, tell stories, cry, laugh, and celebrate the life of a sister who has just died. Since Carla had been in El Salvador for only four months, the people did not know her well enough for such a memorial service, and Ita was missing the Love that had been more overt during their longer ministry in Chile. She said of Carla, "Already she's a little bit larger than life, a heroine, 'an angel of charity.' I guess it's useless for me to protest that my beat up old friend is an example of God's strength being manifested in our weakness; His goodness and love through our vessels of clay."[17]

While talking about her friend's recent death, she focuses on what God can do with our vessels of clay. During my own walk through hell I learned a great deal about this. Evil cannot control a heart surrendering deeply to Love: it did not control Ita or me. Love moving through a surrendered heart is one of earth's most powerful forces. God alone changes hearts, defeats evil's injustice, and does all of this according to his timeline, not ours.

Love's Rising

It might seem that the dedicated and kindly lives of these four women ended horrifically. Their murderers had left their naked, bruised, violated, and lifeless bodies at that desolate site. Their prophetic work and horrible murder could cause us to doubt Love's saving power. But praying with injustice enables us to see beyond the bleak horror of evil acts. These women made contemplation, especially dark contemplation, an everyday reality. Their prayer enabled them to trust in a Love powerful enough to take crucifixion and make resurrection.

Because God carried me through sexual abuse and life-threatening surgery, and then enabled me to see Love in everything and everyone, I focus on God's power to raise us from our suffering. Because I trust that Love brings goodness out of evil's madness, I revel in the resurrection of these women's spirits.

The profoundly destructive evil rampant in El Salvador in the 1980s that was responsible for the rape and murder of these four women was not the end of their story. The telling and retelling of their stories continue. On key anniversaries people from around the world gather in tiny El Salvador to celebrate the women's lives and timeless, expansive presence. Salvadoran military leaders tried to silence their ministry, but evil was not the final word that night. Since then that dark and barren site has been transformed. A memorial stone and chapel commemorate their sacrifice.

The great-hearted Love of God and these women continues to affect others. During the 1983–84 academic year Cynthia Glavac, an Ursuline sister, teaching in the school where Dorothy Kazel had taught before going to El Salvador, had a dream. In the early part of the dream Dorothy and she were standing at a distance from each other in an undetermined time and setting. "From where I stood I could see that Dorothy was dressed in the modified Ursuline habit and was holding an object in her hand. She then began to walk toward me, and I stood still, watching her approach. When she joined me, Dorothy smiled and without a word gave me what she had been carrying: a large manila folder. The dream abruptly ended as I stretched out my hand and accepted the folder."[18] Cynthia woke up and wondered if it had been a dream or if the events had actually happened. "I strongly sensed Dorothy's presence in my bedroom. I did not feel frightened, as her presence was a gentle, non-threatening one, but I did feel puzzled: what was in the folder I so willingly took from Dorothy?"[19]

Later that morning Cynthia shared the dream with an Ursuline friend, Joanne Gross. After mulling over its meaning for a few days, Cynthia forgot about it for six years. In 1989, when she was considering a doctoral dissertation topic, an Ursuline friend suggested she write Dorothy's biography. When she shared the idea with her friend, Joanne remembered the dream and exclaimed, "The dream, Dorothy was giving you the dissertation in that folder!"[20] Cynthia Glavac trusted Joanne's interpretation of the dream and became Dorothy Kazel's biographer.

This dream illumines the resurrected life of these women, and reveals the Dance's power to take evil and make Love. This focus on resurrection does not minimize the horror of the women's murder. Praying with darkness entails an ever-deeper acknowledgment of iniquity. But resurrection highlights a power in this universe that is greater than evil. This dream reveals something of the women's present state. Dorothy Kazel's gentle and nonthreatening presence filled Cynthia Glavac's room.

As a spiritual director, I have sometimes listened to other people's dreams, and, on a few occasions, these dreams have included the presence of resurrected friends. Whenever directees have talked about these experiences, I have heard a refined tone in their voices. Consider the softest, simplest, most beautiful note you have heard a singer hold for a time. This is something like the pure sound I hear in the presence of a directee's resurrected friend.

Because the quality of Cynthia's experience is so similar to others I have heard, I have no doubt that her dead friend revealed herself in her dream. Likewise, the words Cynthia used to describe the dream sound like other resurrection experiences I have heard. For me Dorothy Kazel's smiling, gentle, and palpable presence put the final nail in the coffin of that evil. For God and those close to God, there is little separation between life, death, and resurrection, and contemplation reveals all three.

Rarefied Love

Have you ever experienced the hell of societal injustice? Did you at any point sense God's presence in that agony? Contemplation fosters expectation of Love's presence, but dark contemplation requires heightened vigilance because intense and widespread suffering can greatly hinder awareness of Love's movement.

Dorothy, Ita, Jean, and Maura told their families and friends about the danger that surrounded them; their letters exposed their full consciousness of others' suffering and of their own. The same letters revealed how they surrendered their "vessels of clay" to God when they prayed. In that surrender they experienced God's presence in the midst of that horror. The Love that they met in prayer and life radically transformed them. In them we see Love unto death, a most rarefied Love. Their contemplation reminds us that Jesus suffers, dies, and rises continuously in the darkest times and most heinous crimes. It also helps us trust our own prayer in hard times.

Notes

1 *Boston Globe*, December 5, 1980.

2 Ana Carrigan and Bernard Stone, *Roses in December: The Story of Jean Donovan* (New York: First Run Features, 1982). Gail Pellett, *Justice and the Generals* (New York: First Run/Icarus Films, 2002).

3 *The New American Bible* (New York: Oxford University Press, 2004), 1096.

4 Phyllis Zagano, "Unsettled Business, U.S. Women Martyrs of El Salvador," *St. Anthony Messenger* 110, no. 7 (2002): 18.

5 Ibid., 19.

6 Ibid., 20.

7 Jeanne Evans, ed., *"Here I Am, Lord": The Letters and Writings of Ita Ford* (Maryknoll, N.Y.: Orbis Books, 2005), 177.

8 Ibid., 203.

9 Ibid., 226.

10 Ibid., 172.

11 Ibid., 201.

12 Constance FitzGerald, "Impasse and Dark Night," in *Women's Spirituality*, ed. Joanne Wolski Conn (New York: Paulist Press, 1996), 414.

13 Evans, ed., *"Here I Am,"* 201.

14 FitzGerald, *"Impasse,"* 413.

15 Evans, ed., *"Here I Am,"* 177.

16 Ibid., 178.

17 Ibid., 221.

18 Cynthia Glavac, *In the Fullness of Life* (Denville, N.J.: Dimension Books,1996), 14.

19 Ibid.

20 Ibid.

13

Power and Protest

The lives and deaths of the four churchwomen inspire annual nonviolent protests of the School of the Americas (SOA). Beholding God's movement in their life, death, and resurrection prompts me to denounce all violence against women and girls. Contemplating Love makes us more like Love, and causes us to protest that which is not Love.

Nonviolent Protest

The four churchwomen had been dead twenty-two years when their self-sacrifice stirred Moira Kenny, a Sister of Mercy. Her protest of the practices of the School of the Americas (now called Western Hemisphere Institute for Security Cooperation) intensified my contemplation of it, and prompted me to include her in this chapter. Through several phone conversations and some correspondence, I came to know more about her confrontation of this military school.

The School of the Americas, a United States military school, was moved from Panama to Fort Benning in Columbus, Georgia, in 1984. In the 1960s the school began to teach Latin American officers how to maintain internal control and suppress domestic dissent in their respective countries and continued to do so after the move to Fort Benning. Latin American civilians began calling it the "school of coups," and an editorial in *La Prensa*, a Panamanian newspaper, was the first to call it the "school of assassins."[1]

In 1990 fewer than ten people demonstrated against the role this military school had played in the brutality of Latin American dictatorships. Now, thousands attend this November weekend. With eighty-six other resisters Moira peacefully crossed the property line at Fort Benning in November 2002. She had crossed the line onto the fort's property twice before and had been served a "ban and bar" letter; so she knew that a trial and jail sentence could result from the 2002 crossing. Besides, this was the year following the massive destruction of September 11, and much about our approach to security had understandably changed.

Despite all of this, she crossed the line. As she stepped onto the fort's property, several members of the media put microphones in her face and asked what motivated her civil disobedience. Though she understood the role of the media, she remained silent. For her trespassing on army property was a call and a sacred duty, and speaking to the media would have distracted her from that call. Moira's trial statement reflected the role of the churchwomen in her call. "As a sister, my primary reasons for taking part in the annual protest at the SOA is to honor the memory of Maura Clarke, Ita Ford, Dorothy Kazel, and Jean Donovan. They knew the dangers of living in El Salvador yet recommitted themselves to staying with the people, and then were raped and murdered at the hands of SOA graduates."[2]

There it is again: the power of resurrection. Few men and women religious have forgotten what happened to their companions on December 2, 1980, and November 16, 1989. The beginning and end of that horrifically violent decade in El Salvador was marked by the brutal murders of Archbishop Oscar Romero, three nuns, and a laywoman in 1980 and six Jesuits and two laywomen in 1989 by the Salvadoran military forces. They and their companions live on in all of us. When murdered, these women and men became a part of God's protest unto death. Their spirits prompted and fortified Moira's nonviolent resistance years later. Because too many SOA graduates have violated human rights in heinous ways, she is only one of thousands who march annually to close this school.

Since Moira is a Sister of Mercy, we rallied around her as she went to trial. During her trial, sentencing, and six-month imprisonment at the federal prison camp in Bryan, Texas, she received messages from sisters, associates, and coworkers of Mercy from the United Kingdom, Australia, Peru, New Zealand, Newfoundland, El Salvador, and the United States. Many were touched by her sacrificial stand.

After the trial and sentencing, she sent a letter to all of us. She ended that letter with an e-mail she had received from a campus minister at the University of Texas. She did not know this young woman who wrote, "I received and read a copy of your statement to the judge. I was born in El Salvador but moved to the States at the age of five. Though I left my country at an early age, my childhood memories are stained with much fear and images of murder resulting from the terrible conflict in El Salvador. Most people in the States have no idea what kind of suffering and injustice went on then, and still goes on now, all over the world. As for me, I cannot erase the images from my heart or my mind. On this day, my heart is encouraged by your act of loyalty to Jesus Christ."[3]

My entire community and I were concerned as Moira surrendered herself to the authorities for her six-month sentence. Prisons are dangerous places. We were relieved to hear that her incarceration was humane. Those six months had their difficulties, but she never felt threatened. We corresponded a few times, and I was keenly aware that her willingness to go to jail was also the movement of God. Through her, God confronted the policies of this school; contemplation, protest, and resurrection can be one and the same.

Shock and Grief

My awareness of this training center was less focused before Moira's trial. In the courses I taught during the 1980s, I shared my anguish over the massive financial aid the United States government used to support El Salvador's military. I was relieved when the United Nations finally brokered a peace agreement between Salvadoran rebels and the government in 1992. But praying about El Salvador after the peace accords still grieved me.

I was grateful that the savage abuses had stopped, but my

own country had never publicly acknowledged its role in that conflict. Because of increased protests, our government changed the name of the school to its current name, Western Hemisphere Institute for Security Cooperation in 2000, but this change was a superficial one. Unacknowledged guilt and sinfulness can harm the vitality of an individual or a nation. Human beings suffer greatly when they lose their capacity for contrition. Though God is still close, their hardened hearts prevent them from being aware of Love's nearness. Besides, it is unfair to protest the horrible violence done to us on September 11 without also embracing the equally disturbing assaults we in the United States have mounted against others, like Salvadorans in the 1980s.

Though I was aware of the movement to close the school, Moira's decision to walk onto the Fort Benning property intensified my concentration on this annual protest. Her decision to cross the line and endure the resulting jail sentence forced me to focus more intently on the role of the United States in El Salvador's horror. After one phone conversation with Moira, I looked at the SOA Watch website. I wanted to see how many Salvadoran military leaders had graduated from the School of the Americas. Imagine my shock when I realized that every infamous name with which I was familiar was on that list. In 2002 Amnesty International U.S.A. did a report on U.S. training of foreign military and police forces. It best summarizes what I discovered on that website. Among those who graduated from the SOA were two of the three killers of Archbishop Romero, ten of the twelve who were responsible for the deaths of 900 civilians in the village of El Mozote, three of the five officers involved in the 1980 rape and murder of the U.S. churchwomen, and nineteen of the twenty-six soldiers linked to the murder of the Jesuits.[4]

A Truth Commission

In 1993, after the United Nations brokered peace accords between the Salvadoran government and the rebels, it published its report on the atrocities committed in El Salvador in the 1980s. *From Madness to Hope: The 12-Year War in El Salvador* assessed the crimes committed by the armed forces and their death squads and those enacted by the Salvadoran rebel group (Farabundo Marti National Liberation Front—FMLN). The report recorded 22,000 testimonies of brutality from 1980 to 1991, and it exposed a truth that many suspected despite the political spin of our government. Those giving testimony attributed 95 percent of the violence to agents of the state, whether military or paramilitary, and 5 percent to rebel groups.[5]

The commission members found that much of the violence originated from a mind-set that viewed political opponents as subversives and enemies. Too many people who differed with the government were eliminated with no access to the rule of law. Inhabitants of areas where guerrillas operated were automatically suspected of harboring them. The brutal torture and murder of hundreds of men, women, children, and elderly people in the village of El Mozote on December 11 and Los Toriles on December 12 in 1981 were examples of the military's counterinsurgency policy.[6]

Contemplating Roy Bourgeois

I have written that Love takes death and makes resurrection in its own time. Love's timing, however, is radically different than ours. Because we understandably want evil vanquished within our own timelines, we sometimes miss this movement of God. In 2002 Moira Kenny crossed the line onto Fort Benning's property to honor the sacrifice of four little-known women in 1980. In 2006 Roy Bourgeois, a Maryknoll priest, led thousands in a peaceful protest march to the fort's gates to commemorate the murder of six Jesuits, their two housekeepers, and so many others by El Salvadoran military during that period. The timing of Love's reversals seldom matches our time frames, but its reversal of evil always surpasses our expectations. After Moira's stand, I began to contemplate Roy Bourgeois, the founder of the campaign to suspend and investigate SOA. Visiting the School of the Americas on his own in the summer of 1990, Bourgeois found it overrun with Latinos in jungle fatigues and Salvadoran soldiers at target practice with U.S. instructors. As he watched paper targets made of people's silhouettes being shot at on the firing range, he suddenly pictured the six Jesuits and their two housekeepers who had been massacred seven months earlier. Like many of us, he had seen the photographs of their dead bodies with the brains of some spilled out onto the grass next to their heads.

The horror of this recollection was so vivid, Bourgeois nearly cried. "As I listened to the gunfire, I thought about how few Americans know what goes on here. I realized this is where I belong. This is where it all starts, where the blood trail [in Latin America] begins."[7] He immediately rented a small, run-down apartment only thirty yards from the entrance to Fort Benning. Bourgeois then called a friend, Charles Liteky, to join him for a hunger fast at Fort Benning on Labor Day, 1990. Bourgeois had won a Purple Heart and Liteky a Medal of Honor for their service in Vietnam. These men loved their country enough to challenge it to act justly.[8]

They, along with eight protesters, joined those already objecting to the policies of the Reagan and Bush administrations in Central America. Members of the U.S. Congress and many citizens had been criticizing our role in Central American economies and civil wars for years. Much could be said about the role of the United States in El Salvador during that period, but I wish to focus on one example of our country's complicity in the horror of El Salvador in the 1980s.

Major Gordon Martel had said that a graduate "who leaves here [SOA] and commits atrocities does so in spite of the SOA, not because of it." Another SOA spokesman, Major Jack Rail, had claimed, "We place serious emphasis on human rights. It's beyond our control what happens when Salvadorans go back to their country."[9] Because former students claimed to have read torture manuals while being instructed at the school, leaders of SOA Watch and some congressional leaders did not believe the majors and were searching for this manual. Finally, in 1996, when the Pentagon realized that Congressman Joseph Kennedy had obtained one of the torture manuals, they went public with selected excerpts from the manuals that were used at SOA from 1982 to 1991. They did it on a Friday night after the news shows had completed their programming. These U.S. Army Intelligence manuals used in the training of Latin American military officers advocated executions, tortures, blackmail, and other forms of coercion against insurgents.[10] The school used seven questionable manuals and distributed approximately a thousand others through U.S. training teams in Latin America.

As more truth became public, the number of participants in the November protest grew. In 1996 more than four hundred people came to Columbus, Georgia, and called for the closing of this school. Each year since then, some have crossed the line onto Fort Benning's property, knowing these few steps could earn them a trial and jail sentence. I call this God's protest and resurrection too. With Abraham Heschel, I believe that God is intimately involved in the affairs of human beings. Love "is never neutral, never beyond good and evil, [and] always partial to justice."[11] The Love that I meet when I pray evokes a spirituality of protest among us and uses our dissent to transform injustice, even in its most horrific forms.

As I wrote about God's protest, I once again registered my own. I e-mailed Representative Mike Ferguson and asked him to co-sponsor HR 1707. This legislation about the SOA was introduced in March 2007 by Representative James McGovern. It calls for the suspension of operations at SOA/WHISC and the investigation of torture and human rights abuses that are associated with this military training school. I asked my own representative to join the innumerable bipartisan cosponsors of this bill. A similar bill (HR 3368) was introduced again by Representative James McGovern from Massachusetts in November 2011.

Resurrection and the Four Churchwomen

Disturbing the Peace is a well-researched and finely written biography about Roy Bourgeois, a Maryknoll priest, and his efforts to confront the repressive role of the United States in

Latin America during the last century. On the front cover, we see him carrying a white cross.[12] During their solemn processions at the SOA protest weekend each November, thousands carry crosses like his with the names of Latin Americans who had been violently murdered by their military leaders, many of whom had been trained at the School of the Americas. When each name is read publicly in their hours-long solemn procession, the protesters cry out, "Presente." The presence of those who were presumably silenced lives on in that powerful procession. In that weekend of teach-ins, dramas, and silent procession at Fort Benning, the living and dead cry out, "Let us close the School of the Americas."

The white cross that Roy Bourgeois carries in the procession has a special way of proclaiming resurrection. He knew Ita Ford personally, though not well, and carries her white cross as he marches at the front of thousands. There they are again! Four women, whom Salvadoran military leaders tried to silence, take up their crosses and rise to lead protesters. Who says God is impotent? Resurrected spirits possess Love's eternal might. These women inspire many, and will not cease their protest until the School of the Americas is closed or completely renewed.

They also resurrected me. Because I have prayed about the rape, murder, and resurrection of these four women for more than thirty years, I assumed this chapter would be the easiest. Was I mistaken! Contemplating the horror of El Salvador in the 1980s well enough to write about it was more unnerving than I had imagined, so I wrote this section gradually. If I was to remain sane while attending to God's movement within injustice, I had to follow her plan and schedule. Contemplation is seldom time efficient, but it is always transforming.

God knows me better than I know myself. I had dealt with every imaginable aspect of my own molestation as I walked through three exceedingly painful years. Then, two decades later, Love used this chapter to heal me further. I first detected God's healing designs on Monhegan while watching *Roses in December* and *Justice and the Generals*, two videos about the churchwomen.[13] These videos included the gory details of the women's disinterment. Though it took time for me to realize this, as I observed their lifeless, filthy, and abused bodies, I cowered once more before my rape and its power.

My inability to protect myself as a child followed me into middle-aged adulthood. Though focused on the churchwomen, I soon realized Love was using their sacrifice to heal me further, and their resurrection to intensify mine. I had been experiencing the joy, light, freedom, and Love that accompany our experience of resurrection for years, but had little awareness of its power. Evil still blinded me to resurrection's might.

Love's Power and Protest

Because evil was too graphic and rampant in the videos, and because I am so receptive on Monhegan, I had to stop watching the videos. In the solitude of my apartment there, the evil of my abuse was affecting me again, and I was cowering before everything. Then one night my awareness of the evil done to those women and to me even began to distort reality. For an hour or so I feared that my writing about the violence of Salvadoran military leaders would cause them to find me and treat me like the churchwomen. Thankfully I recognized this distortion, called a few friends, and became less fearful. Then I sat on my porch under Monhegan's starry sky and prayed. Gradually Love's power replaced rape's oppression. Unlike evil, this Dance was both strong and gentle. Love said something like, "I sustain this night sky, and I will defeat evil's power over you." At the same time I felt Love flowing through my body and strengthening me. Peace engulfed me, the cowering left, I went to bed, and slept soundly.

Since then God has used different experiences to empower me further. Most have been simpler but always liberating. Then, as I finished the last section of this chapter, Love drew me to Violence Against Women, a conference presented at the United Nations on March 1, 2011. This was not one of God's gentle attractions. No, God was adamant as he gripped my heart and propelled me toward Manhattan. If I did not get to that conference, there would be no peace between us.

At the symposium Carol Rittner, a Sister of Mercy, spoke about rape being used as a weapon of war. Lee Ann De Reus and Roselyn Constantino, both professors at Penn State Altoona, talked respectively about the unspeakable torture, rape, and murder of women and girls in the Democratic Republic of Congo and in Guatemala.

Diedre Mullan, a Sister of Mercy and the conference coordinator, began the conference by telling us that in the past few weeks a fourteen-year-old Bangladeshi girl had been sentenced to one hundred public lashes. Hena Begum, also called Hena Akhter, was accused of having an affair with Mahbub Khan, her cousin, and even though this punishment had been recently outlawed in Bangladesh, she was sentenced to it under Sharia law. Her family said she was not having an affair but had been raped by her cousin.

One minute I knew nothing about Hena Begum, and the next minute I was profoundly saddened and angered by the horrific torture and murder of this girl. When I arrived home I surfed the internet and found one photograph of Hena as an attractive, smiling youth and another of her as a near-dead girl wrapped in a blanket. Hena had become unconscious after eighty lashes, died a few days later, and was buried on January 31, 2011. Like others on the internet, I was appalled at the evil done to Hena Begum.

This time I did not cower before appalling violence. As I contemplated both photographs, I felt a power that was not of my own making. Love's movement within me was stronger than before; God became a supple yet unyielding pressure that filled my entire body and pressed against my skin. As I sat erect in front of the computer, a resolute "No" welled up from within me. This inner force made of my entire body an outstretched arm with a fist at its apex. God was this inner might, and both of us were protesting rape and violence against all women and girls.

I also found myself saying "NO" to the male domination that subtly or blatantly pervades societies and religions. Scripture tells us that women and men are made in the likeness of God, so beliefs about male superiority have nothing to do with Love. Roman

Catholicism, my faith tradition, is only one of the religions that has a long way to go before its theology and practices reflect God's way of seeing in this area. The domination of one person over another, whether through thought, word, or deed, fosters a belief system that can lead to the brutal torture and murder of someone like Hena Begum. Because any form of domination can lead to violent behavior, I cannot help but wonder about the relationship between my church's patriarchal tradition and the horrific pedophilia crisis that is presently affecting it in so many countries.

God has used the murder of the churchwomen and of Hena Begum to change my powerlessness into protest. Sometimes Love's conversions are so gradual that we hardly notice them. Though I was unaware of it, God had been kneading my powerlessness over rape's destruction for years. But I could not miss these recent changes. Sometimes God's power wells up from my depth, and my entire body becomes an outstretched arm with a fist at its apex. At other times God's power is gentler, but no less firm, within me. As my body becomes an arm reaching upward, my hand opens up and reaches out to everything and everyone. Love's might then seeps through my porous palm, arm, and body. This power that I experience may have a uniquely feminine dimension, but this wide open hand is a newer awareness. God will reveal more to me about her strength in this area, and I can wait. God knows better than I how to vary Love's powerful assertions.

Though I know the most painful and overwhelming aspects of my healing ended when I awoke from brain surgery in 1991, only God knows the subtler dimensions of future healing. But I am certain about one thing. Whether my "No" is vehement or gentle, it is God's might that moves within me and protests violence against women and girls.

Contemplating Resurrection

On the night of December 2, 1980, evil seemed invincible. When I was a child, it seemed that way to me too. But now I see it differently. This chapter adamantly claims that, despite so much evidence to the contrary, Love and its resurrected power are the sole invincible force in this universe. Love took the dead body of Jesus and resurrected a global and cosmic Christ. Love embraced the lifeless bodies of four churchwomen and created annual protests of the School of the Americas in which thousands participate. The churchwomen's resurrected power is also intensifying mine; their protest is enabling mine. I cry out against what society and religion did to Hena Begum and what they do to many women and children on a daily basis. I also emphasize that Love is an eternal force that reverses the most despicable actions. From the ashes of cruelty, God uses protest to resurrect justice, though not in human time frames. I stake everything on Love's might.

Have you ever prayed with your horror over injustice and watched for God's response to this prayer? Contemplation changes us; praying during hard times changes us profoundly. Slowly, it quells our worst fears, heals our deep wounds, and stirs resistance to society's harshness. Contemplation kindles our untamed Love and enflames our protest of that which is not Love. All of this is resurrection. We have only begun to explore our innately human capacity for contemplation and the resurrection power it fosters. Beholding everything, everyone, and the untamed Love that moves through them, makes us ever more like Love itself. We desperately need to contemplate God, so God can empower us to reject evil and evolve a more just species.

Notes

1 James Hodge and Linda Cooper, *Disturbing the Peace* (Maryknoll, N.Y.: Orbis Books, 2004), 143.

2 Trial Statement of Sister Moira Kenny, January 28, 2003.

3 E-mail sent to Moira Kenny, RSM.

4 *Unmatched Power, Unmet Principles* (New York: Amnesty International USA, 2002), 43.

5 B. Belisario, chair, *From Madness to Hope: The 12-Year War in El Salvador* (U.N. Security Council: Report of the Commission on the Truth for El Salvador, IV, A, S/25500, 1993), 43.

6 Ibid., IV, C, 1.

7 Hodge and Cooper, *Disturbing the Peace*, 133.

8 Ibid., 134.

9 Ibid., 165.

10 Ibid., 163–66.

11 Abraham Heschel, *The Prophets* (New York: HarperPerennial, 2001), 298.

12 Hodge and Cooper, *Disturbing the Peace.*

13 Ana Corrigan and Bernard Stone, *Roses in December: The Story of Jean Donovan* (New York: First Run Features, 1982) and Gail Pellet, *Justice and the Generals* (New York: First Run/Icarus Films, 2002).

14

An Ode to Contemplation

For years I searched for a book that highlighted contemplation's vast and deep story; then, without realizing it, I began writing my own version. This is a story of contemplative transformation. Our untamed God is my protagonist, and the plot thickens as Love dances us wildly and makes us more like itself. Then, by story's end, contemplation seals God's words on our hearts: "All shall be well, and all shall be well, and all manner of thing shall be well."[1]

Becoming Who and What We Contemplate

Contemplation transforms us into whom and what we contemplate. Gradually, our seeing, acting, and loving become more like God's seeing, acting, and loving. What a story! At some point our gazing ceases to be something we do and becomes who we are. We no longer contemplate Love; rather we become contemplatives who are immersed in Love and its wildly free Dance. Since the world is saturated with God, contemplation plunges us into the world's joy and pain. Transformation—immersion—saturation: do you know a better drama?

The drama intensifies as God turns life's most gutsy stuff—desire, vulnerability, suffering, and rising—into Love. Teilhard de Chardin sings about matter's holiness; Brian Swimme dances with the sun, moon, and chlorophyll; four churchwomen rise from death to lead protests; and I rise with them from brain surgery into a Love that holds us all. Finally as limitless Love rubs against limited love we become convinced that "All shall be well." Slowly, oh so slowly, contemplation makes us more like Love.

"All Manner of Thing Shall Be Well"

Because the medieval period was a harsh time, Julian of Norwich had ample reason to mistrust and interrogate God about his promise that "All shall be well, and all shall be well, and all manner of thing shall be well."[2] In Chapter 9 I explained how, after twenty years of questioning, God calmed her pained confusion by saying, "What is impossible for you is not impossible for me. I shall preserve my word in everything, and I shall make everything well."[3] She finally understood that human beings cannot comprehend but can trust God's words that everything will be well.

When comparing Julian's early and shorter work to her longer and more mature text, we experience a seasoned optimism and serenity that flows through the latter. At the end of the longer book, she asks to know the Lord's meaning in his revelations about Love, and her lyrics about his response move us many centuries later. "Know it well, love was his meaning. Who reveals it to you? Love. What did he reveal to you? Love. Why does he reveal it to you? For love. Remain in this, and you will know more of the same. But you will never know different, without end."[4] Her mature writing sees Love as the sole invincible and all-embracing force in the universe, and this insight of hers uplifts us.

The contemplation that fostered Julian's optimism and serenity was seldom a feel-good type of prayer. Her pondering involved compassionate listening to suffering, unswerving questioning of God, sensitive attention to God's response, and poetic writing about unconditional Love. As we read *Showings*, we sense tension, and even friction, as limited love rubs against limitless Love. Engaging God's suffering in the world is never a placid sort of prayer, but she engages it so faithfully that God's conviction about the wellness of everything rubs off onto her. The friction of her long contemplative Dance created a manuscript that eventually swelled with optimism. Thomas Merton wrote, "Nowhere in all Christian literature are the dimensions of her Christian optimism excelled."[5]

Julian's contemplation of Love, not rose-colored glasses, enabled her to see a little more like God sees and brought buoyancy and serenity to her writing. A prolonged prayer life does the same for us. As our contemplative attitude grows stronger, we trust God's movement amidst everything, even when this movement is subtle. Contemplating Love and its words elicits optimism and serenity. Gradually, our lives can reflect the words, "All shall be well."[6]

My Serenity

I awoke from brain surgery with a hope and serenity that I never could have predicted. I have written that joy and gratitude overwhelmed me, yet deep peace also accompanied them. Because so much infirmity could have caused negative emotions, I knew the calm that enveloped me was sheer gift.

An awareness that all would be well pervaded my consciousness and generated a tranquillity that has lasted for twenty years. But, like Julian, I am never looking at life through rose-colored glasses. My walk through hell obliterated any rosy tint my vision might have once had, so I now know that life sometimes becomes hell. The evil of sexual abuse no longer controls my mind and spirit, but I believe my body still carries the effects of its once poisonous presence. In order to keep the chronic pain of fibromyalgia at bay and to function rather normally with deficits related to brain surgery, I must work with my body for a minimum of four hours each day. If I stretch muscles, exercise eyes, strengthen legs, prepare food, rest my brain, all on a daily basis, I can live a somewhat typical life. But Love, not physical limitation, fascinates me, and these time-consuming limits pale before the loving communion I see and the serenity I experience.

The coupling of Love and limitation perpetuates tranquillity in me. Now, whenever I push my brain or body beyond their capacity, my thoughts and words become jumbled or I experience pain so severe that I cannot function. So I have become accustomed to one speed—slow. There are times when I wish my body and brain could move faster, but slowness fosters precious gifts. As my body diminishes, my contemplative mind and heart grow stronger. So I now live more contemplatively than when I could move faster. I accomplish fewer tasks, but experience more tranquillity than anxiety. Hopefully, this peacefulness brings more wisdom to what I do accomplish.

The peace that ensues from my contemplative attitude is not of my doing; it is total gift from a magnanimous Giver. Whenever I am fooled into thinking that serenity is a possession rather than a gift, others' limitations or my own become pronounced, and Love reminds me of my reliance on it. Contemplation has plunged me into the world's pain and joy and reminds me that Love moves the universe. When life humbles me enough, I contemplate Love more sensitively. Once again I trust Love's words, "All shall be well," see a little more like God, and know that we all, in Merton's words, "shine like the sun."

A Mystical Quality of Earth

With sweeping changes in communication, widespread cries for democracy, global disruptions in weather patterns, extensive use of violence, and so many destabilized economies, we are surely in flux and may be immersed in another evolutionary leap. I leave the science and significance of this instability to those who are more knowledgeable in these areas, and contemplate a spiritual dimension of this all-embracing insecurity.

We humans have evolved from being hunter-gatherers, villagers, merchants, scientists, and industrialists to being global communicators; what extraordinary leaps we have made. Near the end of Chapter 2 I used a quote from Thomas Berry to highlight the powers that an evolving universe has given us. I include the same quote here to underscore the importance of our spiritual gifts. Berry says the human species is "a mystical quality of the earth, a unifying principle, an integration of the various polarities of the material and the spiritual, the physical and the psychic, the natural and the artistic, the intuitive and the scientific. We are the unity in which all these inhere."[7] What an amazing creation we are!

Yet, as a species, we seem unable to integrate these powers. We are scientifically advanced but cannot live peaceably with each other and earth. Our loving ways enhance the lives of many, and our destructive tendencies harm others grievously. We have difficulty blending our physical, mental, psychological, and spiritual powers, so we are surely an evolutionary work in process. Sometimes our Love is terribly deficient, because we forget that Love is a gift from a magnanimous Giver.

This entire book revolves around earth's sacred dimension and Love's ability to unify everything and everyone, all of which I was shown during anesthetized sleep. The challenges that we face as a species are now earth-size and soul-size, but, as a species, we have only begun to rely on our spiritual powers.

Contemplating Love just might strengthen us, so that we can respond once again to God's great summons. Without contemplating unconditional and infinite Love, I cannot imagine how we will find the strength of soul needed to deal with the threats that are around and within us. Julian's experience of limitless Love rubbing against her limited love caused her to call us to contemplation. "For our Lord wants to have the soul converted to contemplation of him and of all his works in general. For they are most good, and all his judgments are easy and sweet, bringing to great rest the soul which is converted from contemplating men's blind judgments to the judgments, lovely and sweet, of our Lord God."[8]

God's judgments are far gentler than the judgments of humankind; contemplating Love creates gentler, more restful human beings, and makes us more like Love itself. Without Love human beings die inside. Without contemplating the Love that dances everything and everyone, we may destroy our species and much of earth. Will this happen? I hope not, but one final story underscores the significance of contemplating Love.

An Ode to Love

Long ago Love created an evolving universe, became immersed in its galaxies, and, after much unfolding, embraced planet earth. Untamed Love called everything Dance, because it flowed so mutually with Love's deepest rhythms. All things made merry in God's wildly free and jubilant Dance.

Then Love evolved a human species. Creation celebrated its new Dance partners, because human beings unified all aspects of the universe within themselves. They were also blessed with a special gift. Humans could contemplate God's presence everywhere; God and God's creatures rejoiced as mortals reveled in earth's communion.

For a time humans danced harmoniously with their gifts. Then creation's vastness frightened humans; their own powers distracted them; and they forgot that all is gift. They ignored their spiritual depth and no longer contemplated Love's music. They controlled creation rather than dancing it and failed to see the consequences.

Then climates changed; storms intensified; droughts multiplied; food dwindled; poverty spread; disease mushroomed; violence escalated; and society crumbled. Earth suffered greatly; many species died; and humans died too, by the billions. Those who survived were traumatized, and their communities were nearly shattered. God agonized.

But Love uses suffering, especially great suffering, to re-create everything and everyone. Earthwide suffering wakened surviving mortals from their fearful control, and they called out for mercy. Life was harsh, so humans began to rely on each other, on other species, and on Love once again. When they saw that Love had held them securely, even while they looked the other way and let much of earth die, they were humbled.

God's magnanimity evoked sorrow, and resilience flowed from death's ashes. Humans contemplated Love again, as they had before fear nearly destroyed earth. As they contemplated Love, people rose up and gradually became a little more like Love.

Because human beings began to celebrate rather than control

earth's Dance, the glory of creation was apparent to them once more. As humans contemplated all things, earth could enjoy its communion and was again filled with awe. Love's untamed melody danced rocks, flowers, birds, children, women, and men, and all bowed before Love, the Dancer of them all. God said, "All shall be well." Love convinced creation that it held everything and everyone securely and forever.

Notes

1 Julian of Norwich, *The Showings of Julian of Norwich*, ed. Denise N. Baker (New York: W. W. Norton, 2005), 39.

2 Ibid.

3 Julian of Norwich, *Julian of Norwich Showings*, trans. Edmund Colledge and James Walsh (New York: Paulist Press, 1978), 342.

4 Ibid.

5 Thomas Merton, *Mystics and Zen Masters* (New York: Farrar, Straus and Giroux, 1993), 142.

6 Julian of Norwich, *Showings*, ed. Baker, 47.

7 Thomas Berry, *The Great Work* (New York: Bell Tower, 1999), 174–75.

8 Julian of Norwich, *Julian of Norwich*, trans. Colledge and Walsh, 198.

Bibliography

Amnesty International USA. *Unmatched Power, Unmet Principles*. New York: Amnesty International USA, 2002.

Barry, William. *God and You*. New York: Paulist Press, 1987.

Barry, William, and William Connolly. *The Practice of Spiritual Direction*. New York: Seabury Press, 1982.

Berry, Thomas. *The Great Work*. New York: Bell Tower, 1999.

Berry, Thomas, and Brian Swimme. *The Universe Story*. New York: Harper Collins, 1992.

Betancur, Belisario, chairperson. *From Madness to Hope: The 12-Year War in El Salvador. United Nations Truth Commission*. Truth Commission Digital Collection, 1993.

Brooks, Paul. *Rachel Carson: The Writer at Work*. San Francisco: Sierra Club Books, 1989.

Carrigan, Ana, and Bernard Stone. *Roses in December*. New York: First Run Features, 1982.

Conroy, Maureen. *Experiencing God's Tremendous Love*. Neptune, N.J.: Upper Room Spiritual Center, 2009.

DeGrandpre, Richard. *Ritalin Nation*. New York: W. W. Norton, 1999.

Evans, Jeanne, ed. *"Here I Am, Lord": The Letters and Writings of Ita Ford*. Maryknoll, N.Y.: Orbis Books, 2005.

FitzGerald, Constance. "Impasse and Dark Night." In *Women's Spirituality: Resources for Christian Development*, edited by Joanne Wolski Conn. New York: Paulist Press, 1996.

Fontana, Marian. *A Widow's Walk*. New York: Simon and Schuster, 2005.

Glavac, Cynthia. *In the Fullness Of Life*. Denville, N.J.: Dimension Books, 1996.

Hagerty, Barbara Bradley. *Fingerprints of God*. New York: Riverhead Books, 2009.

Heschel, Abraham. *The Prophets*. New York: HarperPerennial, 2001.

Hodge, James, and Linda Cooper. *Disturbing the Peace*. Maryknoll, New York: Orbis Books, 2004.

Hyde, Kerrie. *Gifted Origins to Graced Fulfillment*. Collegeville, Minn.: Liturgical Press, 2001.

Ignatius of Loyola. *The Spiritual Exercises of Saint Ignatius.* Translated and with commentary by George Ganss, S.J. Chicago: Loyola University Press, 1992.

Julian of Norwich. *The Showings of Julian of Norwich.* Edited by Denise N. Baker. New York: W. W. Norton, 2005.

Julian of Norwich. *Julian of Norwich Showings*. Translated by Edmund Colledge and James Walsh. Classics in Western Spirituality. New York: Paulist Press, 1978.

Komp, Diane, M.D. *A Window to Heaven.* Grand Rapids, Mich.: Zondervan, 1992.

Merton, Thomas. *Conjectures of a Guilty Bystander*. New York: Doubleday, 1966.

———. *The Intimate Merton.* Edited by Patrick Hart and Jonathan Montaldo. San Francisco: Harper San Francisco, 1999.

———. *Mystics and Zen Masters.* New York: Farrar, Straus and Giroux, 1967.

———. *A Search for Solitude.* San Francisco: Harper San Francisco, 1997.

McGinn, Bernard. *The Foundations of Mysticism*. New York: Crossroad, 1991.

Mooney, Christopher. *Teilhard de Chardin and the Mystery of Christ.* New York: Harper and Row, 1966.

Moore, Thomas. *Dark Nights of the Soul*. New York: Gotham, 2004.

Oliver, Mary. *New and Selected Poems.* Boston: Beacon Press, 1992.

Pellet, Gail. *Justice and the Generals*. New York: First Run/Icarus Films, 2002.

Ruusbroec, John. *The Spiritual Espousals and Other Works.* Translated by J. Wiseman. Classics of Western Spirituality. New York: Paulist Press, 1985.

Shetterly, Susan Hand. "Really Seeing." *Island Journal* 21 (2005): 39–43. Rockland, Maine: Island Institute.

Silf, Margaret. *At Sea with God*. Notre Dame, Ind.: Sorin Books, 2008.

———. *Close to the Heart.* Chicago: Loyola Press, 1999.

Swimme, Brian. *The Powers of the Universe,* DVD. San Francisco, Calif.: Center for the Story of the Universe, 2004.

———. *The Universe Is a Green Dragon*. Santa Fe, N.M.: Bear & Company, 1984.

Taylor, Jill Bolte. *My Stroke of Insight*. New York: Penguin, 2006.

Teilhard de Chardin, Pierre. *The Divine Milieu*. New York: Harper and Row, 1960.

———. *The Heart of Matter.* New York: Harcourt Brace, 1978.

———. *Toward the Future*. New York: Harcourt, 1975.

Whitney, Helen, and Ron Rosenbaum. *Faith and Doubt at Ground Zero*. New York: PBS DVD Video, 2002.